WEEKDAY SAINTS

WEEKDAY SAINTS

Reflections on Their Scriptures

Mark G. Boyer

WIPF & STOCK · Eugene, Oregon

WEEKDAY SAINTS
Reflections on Their Scriptures

Copyright © 2014 Mark G. Boyer. All rights reserved. Except for brief quotations in critical publications or reviews, no part of this book may be reproduced in any manner without prior written permission from the publisher. Write: Permissions. Wipf and Stock Publishers, 199 W. 8th Ave., Suite 3, Eugene, OR 97401.

Wipf and Stock
An Imprint of Wipf and Stock Publishers
199 W. 8th Ave., Suite 3
Eugene, OR 97401

www.wipfandstock.com

ISBN 13: 978-1-4982-0404-0

Manufactured in the U.S.A.   09/15/2014

The Scripture quotations contained herein are from the *New Revised Standard Version Bible: Catholic Edition* copyright © 1993 and 1989 by the Division of Christian Education of the National Council of the Churches of Christ in the U.S.A. Used by permission. All rights reserved.

Dedicated to my Benedictine teachers
in St. Meinrad School of Theology,
St. Meinrad, Indiana,
1972–1976:
Aurelius Boberek, OSB
Daniel Buechlein, OSB
Ephrem Carr, OSB
Cyprian Davis, OSB
Damian Dietlein, OSB
Colman Grabert, OSB
Harry Hagan, OSB
Columba Kelly, OSB
Sebastian Leonard, OSB
Conrad Louis, OSB
John Machielsen, OSB
Nathan Mitchell, OSB
Matthias Neumann, OSB
Christopher Shappard, OSB
Raymond Studzinski, OSB

Contents

Introduction | xi

January 25
Feast of the Conversion of St. Paul, Apostle | 1

January 26
Memorial of Sts. Timothy and Titus, Bishops | 7

February 22
Feast of the Chair of St. Peter, Apostle | 11

March 19
Solemnity of St. Joseph, Husband of the Blessed Virgin Mary | 15

March 25
Solemnity of the Annunciation of the Lord | 22

April 25
Feast of St. Mark, Evangelist | 28

May 1
Optional Memorial of St. Joseph the Worker | 32

May 3
Feast of Sts. Philip and James, Apostles | 34

May 14
Feast of St. Matthias, Apostle | 38

May 31
Feast of the Visitation of the Blessed Virgin Mary | 42

Friday after the Second Sunday after Pentecost
Solemnity of the Most Sacred Heart of Jesus | 47

Saturday Following the Second Sunday after Pentecost
Memorial of the Immaculate Heart of the Blessed Virgin Mary | 62

June 11
Memorial of St. Barnabas, Apostle | 64

July 3
Feast of St. Thomas, Apostle | 68

July 22
Memorial of St. Mary Magdalene | 72

July 25
Feast of St. James, Apostle | 74

July 29
Memorial of St. Martha | 77

August 10
Feast of St. Lawrence, Deacon and Martyr | 81

August 24
Feast of St. Bartholomew, Apostle | 85

August 29
Memorial of the Martyrdom of St. John the Baptist | 89

September 8
Feast of the Nativity of the Blessed Virgin Mary | 92

September 15
Memorial of Our Lady of Sorrows | 99

September 21
Feast of St. Matthew, Apostle and Evangelist | 103

September 29
Feast of Sts. Michael, Gabriel, and Raphael, Archangels | 107

October 18
Feast of St. Luke, Evangelist | 112

October 28
Feast of Sts. Simon and Jude, Apostles | 116

November 18
Optional Memorial of the Dedication of the Basilica of Sts. Peter and Paul, Apostles | 120

November 30
Feast of St. Andrew, Apostle | 125

December 8
Solemnity of the Immaculate Conception of the Blessed Virgin Mary | 129

December 12
Feast of Our Lady of Guadalupe | 136

December 26
Feast of St. Stephen, First Martyr | 143

December 27
Feast of St. John, Apostle and Evangelist | 147

December 28
Feast of the Holy Innocents, Martyrs | 151

✣ Introduction

The Roman Catholic Church issued its first, modern, one volume Lectionary—a book of biblical texts assigned for every day of the year—in 1970 in response to the Second Vatican Council's call for a greater fare of Scripture during Mass. A three-year Sunday cycle of biblical texts were presented in that book along with a two-year weekday cycle of texts. Neither of those includes the texts for specific saints' memorials, feasts, and solemnities. By the time the Lectionary was revised and published between 1998 and 2002 it had grown to four volumes which provide even more of a richer fare of God's word for his people. Because of the revision, many weekday celebrations of saints were assigned texts that were not in the 1970 Lectionary.

Because of its success, many other Christian denominations adopted and adapted the Lectionary to fit their own needs. So, Anglicans, Episcopalians, Presbyterians, Methodists, Lutherans, and many others began to use the Lectionary, which was published in various volumes and mandated or made optional, depending on the Christian denomination. Thus, as is often the case, in churches using a Lectionary worshipers will hear the same biblical text on a given Sunday; all that may differ is the English translation used. Furthermore, in those churches that have weekday services, the same Scripture texts may be heard along with the same celebration of a saint.

During some years in the Roman Catholic Church, particular solemnities and feasts of the Lord, the Blessed Virgin Mary, and some others which fall on Sunday take precedence over a Sunday, particularly one in the Season of Ordinary Time. According to the Introduction to the *Lectionary for Mass*, "For solemnities and feast of the General Roman Calendar proper readings are always assigned" (84.1). There are also solemnities, feasts, memorials, and optional memorials (the four hierarchical rankings) that interrupt the weekday cycle of readings; these solemnities, feasts, memorials, and optional memorials are never celebrated on a Sunday. Solemnities and feasts always have proper Scripture texts. However, some memorials and

Introduction

optional memorials during the weekdays have proper first readings and/or proper gospel passages that are to be read on the memorial or optional memorial. According to the Introduction to the *Lectionary for Mass*, these "proper readings are given for celebrations of the saints, that is, biblical passages about the saint or the mystery that the Mass is celebrating" (83).

This volume provides reflections on these proper biblical passages which "must take the place of the weekday readings for the same day" (83). Any member of a Christian congregation marking the celebration of a saint on a weekday will find these reflections on the Scripture texts assigned to a particular saint very helpful.

Using the Book

This book is designed to be used by individuals for private study and prayer and by ministers for study, prayer, and preaching. A five-part exercise is offered for every solemnity, feast, memorial, and optional memorial that occurs during the liturgical year on a weekday and has proper readings. In each exercise I bring together the study of the Bible and the praying of the Bible. The result is a biblical spirituality that is the foundation for the church's proclamation and preaching during the liturgical year.

1. A title is given to the exercise for the day. If two choices are presented for Scripture texts, these are numbered as (1) and (2). The title is followed by the name of the solemnity, feast, memorial, or optional memorial. Then, the notation (biblical book, chapter, and verses) for the reading is given. I recommended that the reader find the passage in his or her Bible and read it in its context.

2. A few short verses of Scripture are taken from the reading provided in the Lectionary for the solemnity, feast, memorial, or optional memorial.

3. A reflective study follows the Scripture selection. The reflection critiques the passage by applying modern forms of biblical criticism and gives it a context for understanding it. As it offers the individual and the minister valuable background and contextual information concerning the reading, the reflection yields new perspectives for personal study on and suggestions for application of the biblical passage for the day.

Where appropriate I quote from the *Catechism of the Catholic Church*. The quotations are meant to help contextualize the biblical passages. At the end of a quote from the *Catechism*, the reference is indicated by the paragraph number in parentheses.

Introduction

Throughout the reflections, I use the masculine pronoun for God, LORD, LORD God, etc. I am well aware that God is neither male nor female, but in order to avoid the repetition of nouns over and over again, I employ male pronouns, as they are also used in the Lectionary and throughout most biblical translations.

4. The reflection is followed by a question for personal meditation. The question functions as a guide for personal appropriation of the message of the Scripture passage. People who like to journal may find the question appropriate for that activity. The minister can use the question as a basis for a sermon or brief homily.

5. A prayer summarizes the original theme of the Scripture reading, which was studied and explored in the reflection and which served as the foundation for the meditation. The prayer concludes the daily exercise for the individual or it can be adapted and used as a fitting conclusion to the Universal Prayer during the celebration of Eucharist, the Liturgy of the Hours, or any other type of prayer that may be a part of the weekday observance.

It is my hope that through study and prayer with the saints, the reader will come to a deeper knowledge of and a closer relationship with the One around whom all solemnities, feasts, memorials, and optional memorials turn—the Triune God: Father, Son, and Holy Spirit, who has revealed himself as One through his Word in both the Hebrew Bible (Old Testament) and Christian Bible (New Testament).

Mark G. Boyer
August 6, Feast of the Transfiguration of the Lord

❋ January 25
Feast of the Conversion of St. Paul, Apostle

Bright Light

(1) Acts 22:3–16

Scripture: [Paul said to the people of Jerusalem,] "While I was on my way and approaching Damascus about noon a great light from heaven suddenly shone about me. I fell to the ground and heard a voice saying to me, 'Saul, Saul, why are you persecuting me?'" (Acts 22:6–7)

Reflection: There are three accounts of Paul's conversion in the Acts of the Apostles—9:1–19, 22:3–16, 26:2–18—of which two are provided as options for the first reading for this Feast of the Conversion of St. Paul. All three accounts differ in their details. Furthermore, in his own letters Paul mentions some details of his conversion—1 Corinthians 15:9, Galatians 1:13–17—that differ from those in the Acts. The most dramatic retelling of the event is found in the Acts of the Apostles, written by the same person who authored Luke's Gospel.

In this first option for the first reading, the "great light from heaven" (22:6) indicates God's presence. The repetition of Saul's name echoes that of God's call of Moses, standing before the light of the burning bush. The blindness caused by "the brightness of that light" (22:11) can be understood in two ways: It may be physical, or it may represent Saul's lack of faith in the Jesus of Nazareth he has been persecuting.

Saul's companions "saw the light but did not hear the voice of the one who was speaking" (22:9) to him. So, they led him to Ananias in Damascus, who commands, "Brother Saul, regain your sight!" (22:13) And at that moment, Saul is able to see. He gets up and is baptized.

The Lectionary omits the rest of the story, namely, Saul's trip to Jerusalem, where, while praying in the temple, he falls into a trance and sees Jesus, who tells him to leave the city. The last line illustrates Saul's mission to the Gentiles. Jesus says, "Go, for I will send you far away to the Gentiles" (22:21). This latter detail recalls Isaiah's call in the temple (6:1–13). Just like Jesus has been the light for Saul, so will he be the light for the Gentiles.

This narrative of Saul's conversion must be approached carefully, because it gives the impression that conversion is a once-in-a-lifetime experience. We can conclude that once we have converted to the "Way" (22:4), that is, Christianity, we are finished. However, the contrary is the truth.

Conversion is a lifetime process. The great light continues to flash before us, calling us to further growth and development. For example, the great light of a Bible study group can call us to deeper understanding of the Scriptures. Serving on a parish committee can be a great light that enables us to see the unfounded quality of our criticisms of the group's work. Embracing stewardship of time, talent, and treasure is often a great light revealing that all is gift from a very gracious God, who wills that we share with others what he has entrusted to us; stewardship serves to illumine our cultural presupposition that we have earned or bought whatever we have.

Meditation: What great light has called you to repeated conversion?

Prayer: God of light, you brightened the world with the resurrection of your Son, Jesus Christ, who filled your servant Saul with faith. Shine in our minds and hearts that we may be converted further and serve you ever more faithfully. We ask this through our Lord Jesus Christ, who lives and reigns with you and the Holy Spirit, one God, forever and ever. Amen.

Conversion

(2) Acts 9:1–22

Scripture: "For several days [Saul] was with the disciples in Damascus, and immediately he began to proclaim Jesus in the synagogues, saying, 'He is the Son of God.' Saul became increasingly more powerful and confounded

Feast of the Conversion of St. Paul, Apostle

the Jews who lived in Damascus by proving that Jesus was the Messiah" (Acts 9:19–20, 22).

Reflection: The second option for the first reading for the Feast of the Conversion of St. Paul is the first of three accounts of his conversion in the Acts of the Apostles: 9:1–19, 22:3–16, 26:2–18. While details differ from one account to the next and from references in Paul's own letters, the basic idea remains the same, namely, that Saul, who sought to wipe out Christianity, was converted to it and became its most ardent proponent.

As in the other accounts, God's presence is indicated by a light from heaven. The repetition of Saul's name echoes that of the call of Moses before the light of the non-consumed burning bush. Saul's revelation that he has been persecuting Jesus is paralleled with Ananias' vision that he go to meet Saul at a house on Straight Street. Ananias recounts the rumors about Saul, but obeys after the Lord explains that Saul "is an instrument whom [he] has chosen to bring [his] name before Gentiles and kings and before the people of Israel" (9:15). Jesus explains to Ananias that he will show Saul "how much he must suffer for the sake of [his] name" (9:16).

Ananias finds Saul and tells him that he has been sent to help him regain his sight and "be filled with the Holy Spirit" (9:17), a unique Lukan theme that permeates both Luke's Gospel and his second volume, the Acts of the Apostles. Once Saul's sight is restored, he is baptized, takes food, and regains his strength.

Then, he begins to proclaim the very message he set out originally to destroy: Christianity. He goes to the Jewish synagogues and proclaims that Jesus is the Son of God. Furthermore, he declares that Jesus is the Messiah, Hebrew for "Anointed." In some English translations the Greek word for anointed is used, namely, "Christ." Those who hear Saul are confounded. Before his conversion he was the instrument of death for those who believed that Jesus was the Son of God and Messiah; now he is proclaiming exactly the opposite.

The Lectionary omits the narrative that explains the results of Saul's preaching. The Jews begin a plot to kill Saul, so he must escape, being lowered from the Damascus' city walls in a basket. He goes to Jerusalem, but the disciples there are afraid of him until Barnabas explains how he has been converted. As Saul preaches to the Greeks, they, too, attempt to kill him. So, believers take him to Caesarea and send him off to Tarsus.

In this narrative of Saul's conversion, Luke establishes the pattern that he will use throughout the rest of his stories about Saul. First he goes to the Jews, and when they reject him, he goes to the Gentiles. In other words, we should never stop proclaiming Jesus, even when we are rejected. If some will not listen, then we move on.

Conversion is turning one-hundred eighty degrees. It is the process of going from one belief to another. It begins with changing our minds; it is followed by changes in our behavior. Saul is a good example. He changes his mind about Jesus. At first, being a devoted Jew, he had attempted to eradicate those who followed Jesus. After his experience of the great light, blindness, and baptism, he changes his mind. Unknown to Saul, he discovers that he has been persecuting Jesus. This change in mind results in change in behavior. He no longer preaches against Jesus and his disciples; now, he declares that Jesus is the Son of God and Messiah.

There is a depth to conversion that can be missed easily by contemporary people. It is not about church hopping until we find one that makes us feel good. It is about a radical change that occurs deep down within us because of an encounter with the Father, the Son, or the Holy Spirit. Through reflection, we discover that the Father protected us from harm in an auto accident; this causes us to see God's Fatherly care in many more ways. The change in our behavior is witnessed in driving more carefully—eyes on the road, hands on the steering wheel, cell phone turned off.

We may experience the Son while volunteering at the local soup kitchen. A fellow worker or a homeless person makes us aware that as human beings we are brothers and sisters. More volunteering results; we desire to serve Christ in those suffering from natural disasters—tornados, floods, earthquakes—and find ourselves on the ground ministering to those in need.

An idea or thought sits in our consciousness; it may have come from a newspaper, book, or magazine. It may have come from a biblical passage. We are inspired to do something, and we act on the idea. The Holy Spirit has been at work, changing our minds and changing our behaviors. That is deep conversion; that is the conversion that Saul experienced.

Meditation: What recent experience of deep conversion have you had? What change occurred in your mind and in your behavior?

Feast of the Conversion of St. Paul, Apostle

Prayer: God of St. Paul, through Jesus, your servant and your Son, you called the persecutor of your Church to be its greatest defender. Through revelation, you changed his mind about the Messiah and filled him with the Holy Spirit so that he would proclaim Jesus to be your Son. Bring us to deep conversion, that we may imitate Saul, preaching Jesus as your Son and our Messiah. He lives and reigns with you and the Holy Spirit, one God, forever and ever. Amen.

Go!

Mark 16:15–18

Scripture: [Jesus said to the Eleven,] "Go into all the world and proclaim the good news to the whole creation" (Mark 16:15).

Reflection: Mark's Gospel has three canonical endings, a fact which often comes as a surprise even to avid Bible readers. The original ending occurs at 16:8. At another time, another sentence was added to 16:8, which has come to be known as the shorter ending. At still another time, verses 9 through 20 were added; this is known as the longer ending. Today's pericope is taken from the longer ending of Mark's Gospel which seems to be a summary and combination of the endings of Matthew's Gospel and Luke's Gospel.

The Lectionary omits the introductory verse to today's passage: Jesus "appeared to the eleven . . . as they were sitting at the table; and he upbraided them for their lack of faith and stubbornness, because they had not believed those who saw him after he had risen" (16:14). Then, he told them to go into the whole world and announce the good news to the whole creation.

The passage is chosen for this Feast of the Conversion of St. Paul because, even though he was not one of the eleven, he went into the whole world and proclaimed the good news of salvation. Furthermore, in the churches he established, he baptized and appointed leaders. He cast out demons in the name of Jesus Christ. He handled a deadly snake, and he healed the sick by laying his hands on their heads. In other words, the deeds of Paul recorded in the Acts of the Apostles—and in his own letters—are summarized by the longer ending of Mark's Gospel.

Like Paul, conversion sends us on our way. We hear the command, "Go!" In a culture that does not like change, conversion is the antidote. Jesus had to reproach the eleven for their unbelief and hardness of heart; in other words, he called them to conversion. He called Saul to conversion. He calls us to conversion.

Go, volunteer to take communion to the sick of your parish and to those in nursing homes. Go, sign up to help with disaster relief. Go, spend a few hours in the local soup kitchen, food pantry, or medical clinic. Go, prepare others for baptism through membership on your parish Rite of Christian Initiation team, or go, prepare parents for the baptism of their children. If others are to hear the good news—Jesus died and God raised him—we have to go to wherever and to whomever we are called by God or led by the Holy Spirit.

Meditation: How has a conversion experience sent you to others?

Prayer: Almighty God, you sent your Son into the world to be its salvation. Once he converted Paul, he sent him to announce the good news to all creation. Give us the guidance of the Holy Spirit that we may know the ministry to which you call us and, then, send us with the gospel that Jesus Christ lives and reigns with you and the Holy Spirit, one God, forever and ever. Amen.

✣ January 26
Memorial of Sts. Timothy and Titus, Bishops

Faithfulness

(1) 2 Timothy 1:1–8

Scripture: "Paul, an apostle of Christ Jesus by the will of God for the sake of the promise of life that is in Christ Jesus, to Timothy my beloved child: Grace, mercy, and peace from God the Father and Christ Jesus our Lord" (2 Tim 1:1–2).

Reflection: There is no doubt that Paul had an associate named Timothy. Some of the genuine Pauline letters are sent by Paul and Timothy, such as 2 Corinthians, Philippians, and 1 Thessalonians. Paul identifies Timothy as his co-worker in Romans (16:21) and 1 Thessalonians (3:2). Luke mentions Timothy at least seven times in the Acts of the Apostles, identifying him as a disciple having a Jewish mother and a Greek father (16:1).

However, most biblical scholars do not think that Paul wrote either the first or second letter to Timothy. These letters betray a time long after Paul is dead. They are written in Pauline style and contain many Pauline ideas, but presume a developed church that did not yet exist during Paul's lifetime. It is best to understand Timothy in the letters written to him as any leader of a church near the end of the first century and the beginning of the second century AD.

In today's first option for this Memorial of Sts. Timothy and Titus, the passage, which is proper for the memorial, consists of the first eight verses of the second letter to Timothy. The anonymous author of the letter displays his familiarity with references to Timothy in other biblical literature. In the greeting of the letter, the author refers to Timothy as "my beloved child" (1:2), echoing 1 Corinthians 4:17, where Paul calls him "my beloved and faithful child in the Lord."

The author writes to Timothy, "I am reminded of your sincere faith, a faith that lived first in your grandmother Lois and your mother Eunice and now, I am sure, lives in you" (1:5). In 1 Corinthians 4:17, Paul reminds the Christians in Corinth that he sent Timothy to them to remind them "of [his] ways in Christ Jesus, as [he] teache[s] them everywhere in every church." And in 1 Corinthians 16:10, Paul tells the addressees that Timothy is "doing the work of the Lord just as [he is]." In his letter to the Philippians, Paul tells the believers in Philippi that they know Timothy's worth, that "like a son with a father he has served with [him] in the work of the gospel" (2:22).

Today's passage is presented as a required option for this memorial because it tells Timothy "to rekindle the gift of God that is within [him] through the laying on of [Paul's] hands" (1:6). The laying on of hands is the sign of the sacrament of holy orders today. Since Timothy is designated a bishop, the passage emphasizes his reception of God's "spirit of power and of love and of self-discipline" (1:7). As a bishop, Timothy (any bishop or church leader at the end of the first century) is exhorted by the writer of the letter to remain faithful even if such steadfastness entails "suffering for the gospel" (1:8).

Today, not only do church leaders need to remain faithful, "relying on the power of God" (1:8), but all Christians need to hear this exhortation. In a culture that dictates that one can do whatever he or she feels like, faithfulness to the way of life of the gospel often takes a back seat. Likewise, faithfulness to prayer "night and day" (1:3) has become once a week for an hour on Sunday—if that. Faithfulness in bearing witness to the Lord often means rejection for following a code of ethics that illustrates "a holy calling" (1:9) instead of a greedy one. Celebrating the memorial of Sts. Timothy and Titus serves as a call to all of us to examine our degree of faithfulness.

Meditation: In what specific ways are you faithful to the Christian holy calling?

Prayer: We give thanks to you, Mighty God, for Sts. Timothy and Titus, co-workers of St. Paul, and examples of faithfulness to our Lord Jesus Christ. Make our faith even more sincere; fill us with your Spirit of power, love, and good judgment. We ask this through the same Jesus Christ, your Son,

Memorial of Sts. Timothy and Titus, Bishops

who lives and reigns with you and the Holy Spirit, one God, forever and ever. Amen.

Adult Education

(2) Titus 1:1–5

Scripture: "I [, Paul,] left you [,Titus,] behind in Crete for this reason, so that you should put in order what remained to be done, and should appoint elders in every town, as I directed you . . ." (Titus 1:5).

Reflection: There is no doubt that Paul had an associate named Titus. Some of the genuine Pauline letters mention Titus, especially 2 Corinthians, in which Paul refers to him as his "partner and co-worker" (8:23). In his letter to the Galatians, Paul indicates that he "went up again to Jerusalem with Barnabas, taking Titus along" (2:1). In the same letter, he also indicates that Titus was "a Greek" (2:3).

However, most biblical scholars do not think that Paul wrote the letter to Titus. The letter betrays a time long after Paul is dead. It is written in Pauline style and contains Pauline ideas, but it presumes a developed church that did not yet exist during Paul's lifetime. It is best to understand Titus in the letter written to him as any leader of a church near the end of the first century and the beginning of the second century AD facing false teachers. In other words, the letter presents an orderly way of life that can be applied to any follower of Christ dealing with falsehood.

Today's memorial identifies Titus as a bishop, because in the last verse of the pericope from Paul's letter to Titus, the apostle tells him to "appoint elders in every town" (1:5). Elders, who ultimately come to be known as priests, are appointed as pastors of parishes by bishops. Thus, Titus is identified as a bishop. In fact, in verses not included in this passage, the author mentions the characteristics (1:7–9) of a good "bishop" (1:7). This structure reflects a church well into the second century.

The words addressed to Titus are, fittingly, addressed to us today. All Christians are responsible for advancing "the faith of God's elect" (1:1). We do this primarily through the lives we lead. Later in this letter, the author presents detailed instructions for older men, older women, young men, young women, and slaves.

Also, Christians are responsible for advancing "knowledge of the truth" (1:1). We know this as adult education. We live in a time when many Catholics don't know the basics of their faith. Thus, the study of the *Catechism of the Catholic Church*, the Bible, the sacraments, and other Church documents is essential for understanding our "hope of eternal life that God, who never lies, promised before the ages began" (1:2).

As the author of the letter mentions, this is "the faith we share" (1:4). It is not a personal faith, though belief begins with each individual person. The Church is one, holy, universal, and apostolic. Every Sunday we express that common faith in the Profession of Faith, also known as the Nicene Creed. Without adult education, it is easy for an individual me-and-Jesus attitude to develop instead of a community all-of-us-and-Jesus understanding. Celebrating the memorial of Sts. Timothy and Titus gives all of us the occasion to examine our growth in advancing our faith through our understanding of it.

Meditation: In what specific ways do you live and learn about our common faith?

Prayer: Ever-living God, you never leave your Church unattended, but appoint for her leaders who will guide your people in the one common faith and teach them knowledge of the truth. Raise bishops and priests to serve your Church in faithfulness. Give them the courage to proclaim the revelation of your Word, Jesus Christ, who lives and reigns with you and the Holy Spirit, one God, forever and ever. Amen.

✤ February 22
Feast of the Chair of St. Peter, Apostle

Peter's Successor

1 Peter 5:1–4

Scripture: ". . . [W]hen the chief shepherd appears, you [, elders,] will win the crown of glory that never fades away" (1 Pet 5:4).

Reflection: The Feast of the Chair of St. Peter has nothing to do with a physical chair. The name of the feast refers to the authority of the man who sits in Peter's chair to teach, sanctify, and govern the Church: the pope, the bishop of Rome, the successor of Peter. The passage from the first letter of Peter is chosen for this feast because it portrays the writer of the letter exhorting "the elders . . . to tend the flock of God that is in [their] charge, exercising the oversight, not under compulsion but willingly, as God would have [them] do it—not for sordid gain but eagerly" (5:2). Elders, who ultimately come to be known as bishops in the Church, are told not to lord their authority over those in their charge, but to be "examples to the flock" (5:3).

Today's passage from the first letter of Peter contains the household duties of elders or local Church leaders at the end of the first century or the beginning of the second century AD. Lists of household duties are common in documents written at this time. The anonymous author writes in the name of "Peter, an apostle of Jesus Christ" (1:1), who claims authority to write the letter as "a witness of the sufferings of Christ, as well as one who shares in the glory to be revealed" (5:1).

In the Catholic Church, the pope as Peter's successor serves as head of the universal Church. The bishops, successors of the apostles, are united under the primacy of the pope in order to tend the faithful who have been placed in their care. Teaching or preaching the gospel and maintaining its truth is the primary way the pope and bishops keep the Church united in matters of faith and morals. This teaching role is exercised in ecumenical councils, synods, and pastoral letters.

Both through the bishops of the Church and directly, the pope exercises his sanctifying office. Through prayer and sacraments, the faithful are built into greater unity. This occurs on a parish level under the leadership of priests and deacons and on a diocesan level under the leadership of the local bishop.

And the pope, directly and through the bishops, exercises his governing office through councils, exhortations, and example. This occurs on a parish level under the leadership of the pastor in consultation with a parish council and a finance council. On a diocesan level, the bishop's governing takes place after consultation with a diocesan pastoral council, a presbyteral council, staff meetings, etc. When the chief shepherd, Christ, appears, all hope to win the crown of glory that never fades away.

In a time when the slogan is "No one is going to tell me what to do," the exercise of the papal offices of teaching, sanctifying, and governing are severely criticized because the pope calls Catholics to be different, to stand for religious values. When the secular world gives its assent to a man and woman living together before marriage, the Church, under the leadership of the pope and bishops, calls Catholic couples to abstinence before marriage. When others see no moral problem creating life outside the womb, the Catholic Church witnesses to the natural means of conception. The pope and bishops teach the sacredness of life, as secular culture advocates euthanasia.

The chief shepherd, Christ, is the model the pope strives to emulate. Christ has promised divine assistance to the man who sits in Peter's chair. That gives Catholics a sense of security that they are being taught the truth, that they are being made holy, and that they are being governed by Christ in the person of the pope.

Meditation: In what specific ways have you experienced the teaching, sanctifying, and governing office of the pope either directly or through your local bishop or pastor?

Prayer: Heavenly Father, you bestow the gift of the Holy Spirit upon your Church to assist her leaders in teaching, sanctifying, and governing your people. Guide the vicar of Christ on earth, the pope, with this same Spirit that when the chief shepherd appears, all your people will win the crown of glory that never fades away. We ask this through Christ, our Lord. Amen.

Rock

Matthew 16:13–19

Scripture: [Jesus said to Simon Peter:] ". . . [Y]ou are Peter, and on this rock I will build my church, and the gates of Hades will not prevail against it" (Matt 16:18).

Reflection: When hearing the title of today's feast, the Chair of St. Peter, most people think of a physical chair instead of the authority that the title of the feast indicates. Basically, this is a feast that celebrates the leadership and authority of the papacy. As the successor of Peter, the pope presides over the Church in unity.

The gospel chosen for this feast from Matthew comes from two sources. First, Mark's Gospel is the source for the narrative in the district of Caesarea Philippi. Matthew has changed a number of details to prepare for his additions to the story. Second, Matthew, written around 80 AD, presents what biblical scholars call unique Petrine material, that is, stories that feature Peter that are not found in any other gospel.

Unique Petrine material was created by Matthew or gathered from a source to which he had access in order to re-create the character of Peter found in Mark's Gospel. Peter is characterized as a fool in Mark. Matthew chooses to present him as a leader. So, to Mark's account of Jesus' questioning his disciples as to his identity, Matthew adds the words of Jesus declaring that Peter is the recipient of divine revelation after Peter answers Jesus, "You are the Messiah, the Son of the living God" (16:16).

The Matthean Jesus makes it clear that Peter is the foundation for the church: ". . . [Y]ou are Peter, and on this rock I will build my church, and the gates of Hades will not prevail against it" (16:18). The play on words does not work in the English translation of the Greek text. In Greek, the word "petra" means "rock"; thus, the name "Peter" indicates that the man is the foundation of the church. As most notes in Bibles indicate, Peter is known by his Aramaic name, "Kephas," in the early church. "Kephas" is derived from the Aramaic word for rock, namely, "kepha." In both Greek and Aramaic the word play is obvious, but is missed in English translation. In order to capture the intent of the Matthean Jesus' words, the verse needs to be translated like this: You are Rocky, and upon this foundation I will build my church.

Matthew is the only gospel to use the Greek word "ekklesia" (or "ecclesia"), translated into English as "church." The word does not refer to a building, as it does in contemporary parlance. In Matthew, church is an assembly of people. This community is built on and held together by the Rock, Peter.

Another Petrine passage is added by Matthew. Jesus gives the keys to the kingdom of heaven to Peter. In the ancient world, a key was a sign of authority; it gave its bearer the ability to admit and to keep out. Jesus assures Peter that whatever he binds on earth will be bound in the kingdom; and whatever he loses on earth will be loosed in the kingdom.

The Church has understood this passage to be her basis for continuing the teaching of Jesus for two thousand years, especially concerning matters of faith and morals. As the *Catechism of the Catholic Church*, quoting St. Maximus the Confessor, states, ". . . [A]ll Christian churches everywhere have held and hold the great Church that is here [at Rome] to be their only basis and foundation since, according to the Savior's promise, the gates of hell have never prevailed against her" (834).

Today's feast celebrates the fact that we "believe in one, holy, catholic, and apostolic Church," as we profess in the Nicene Creed, founded by Christ on the Rock (Peter) and presided over by Peter's successor.

Meditation: What does it mean to you to be a member of the one, holy, catholic, and apostolic Church?

Prayer: Father of our Lord Jesus Christ, Simon Peter's profession of faith led your Son to declare him the foundation stone of the Church and to give him the authority to teach your truth. Keep us faithful to the one, holy, catholic, and apostolic Church and grant us admittance to the kingdom, where you live and reign with Jesus Christ and the Holy Spirit, one God, forever and ever. Amen.

✣ March 19
Solemnity of St. Joseph, Husband of the Blessed Virgin Mary

David

2 Samuel 7:4–5a, 12–14a, 16

Scripture: "... [T]he word of the LORD came to Nathan [the prophet]: Go and tell my servant [King] David: Thus says the LORD: Your house and your kingdom shall be made sure forever before me; your throne shall be established forever" (2 Sam 7:4, 16).

Reflection: The short, pieced-together passage for this Solemnity of St. Joseph is part of a much longer discourse given by the prophet Nathan to King David. The king proposes to build a house for God, that is, a temple in Jerusalem into which the ark of the covenant will be placed. However, instead of David building a house for God, the LORD declares that he will build a house, that is, a dynasty, for David.

Biblical theologians refer to this as the "everlasting covenant." God promises David that there will always be a king from David's family ruling in Jerusalem. The promise made to David around 1000 BC continued until 587 BC when the last king of Judah went into Babylonian Captivity. After this, the everlasting covenant became a messianic expectation; God would provide a messiah, who would rescue the people and restore the Kingdom of Judah politically and religiously. Historically, this never happened.

One of the earliest writers about Jesus of Nazareth believes that he is that hoped-for messiah. Around 80 AD, the author of Matthew's Gospel began his book with a "genealogy of Jesus the Messiah, the Son of David, the son of Abraham" (1:1). Joseph, to whom Mary is engaged, is addressed by an angel of the Lord in a dream as a "son of David" (1:20). Thus, the author of Matthew's Gospel presents Jesus as the fulfillment of the messianic expectation ignoring two problems. First, if the Holy Spirit is the father of the child in Mary's womb (1:18), Joseph is not the father and the genealogy back to David does not work. Second, Jesus did not restore the Kingdom of Judah; he died at the hands of the Romans occupying what had once been that nation.

However, if Joseph is understood as the legal father of Jesus, then the author of the first gospel has made his point. Carefully, he declares through the angel of the Lord that Jesus "will save his people from their sins" (1:21). Like the other unexpected people listed in his genealogy, especially the four women (Tamar, Rahab, Ruth, wife of Uriah), the author of Matthew's Gospel proclaims Jesus to be the messiah through whom God fulfills his promise.

The author of Matthew's Gospel understands that God works in ways that people often do not understand, and Joseph, husband of Mary, is one prime example of that. When we hear about someone who has had her cancer disappear unexpectedly, the LORD has fulfilled a promise to heal his people. A marriage that was about to end in divorce may be saved by God through a friend's advice. A woman's alcoholism may provide the Holy One the occasion to draw her closer to himself. We cannot name all the ways God saves his people, but we can declare that the LORD keeps his promise.

Meditation: In what unexplained way has God worked in or through your life to save you or another person?

Prayer: Almighty Father, you raised up Joseph, a righteous man, to be the husband of the Blessed Virgin Mary and the foster father of your Son, Jesus Christ. Grant us the grace to see your saving work in our lives that we may praise your goodness. We ask this through the same Jesus Christ, who lives and reigns with you and the Holy Spirit, one God, forever and ever. Amen.

Righteousness

Romans 4:13, 16–18, 22

Solemnity of St. Joseph, Husband of the Blessed Virgin Mary

Scripture: ". . . [T]he promise that he would inherit the world did not come to Abraham or to his descendants through the law but through the righteousness of faith" (Rom 4:13).

Reflection: "Righteousness" is a very important biblical word, especially for Paul. Righteousness defines a state of being in a healthy relationship with God. In his letter to the Romans, Paul argues that Abraham's trust of God was a response to God's offer of a relationship with him. In accepting the free gift, God declares Abraham righteous apart from the Torah, which had not yet been given to Moses. This enables Paul to conclude that anyone who accepts God's offer of grace with an appropriate response is righteous.

This argument is important for Paul, because he wants to include the Gentiles—non-Jews—among those to whom God has offered righteousness through the resurrection of Jesus Christ from the dead. Jews and Gentiles who accept God's grace and respond through faith that God raised Jesus from the dead are righteous. God has invited them into a healthy relationship with him, and they have responded.

Paul is declaring that God's promise to Abraham was not the result of any works that Abraham did; in other words, Abraham did not earn righteousness. Righteousness was a gift offered to him by God. If righteousness can be earned, then there is no reason for faith, trust in God's reliability. In Pauline understanding, Jesus is the model of trust. He was handed over to death and raised by God. Anyone who believes in the God who raised Jesus from the dead is declared righteous by God.

In the context of this solemnity, the pericope from Paul's letter to the Romans is chosen to highlight the righteousness of St. Joseph. According to Matthew's Gospel, Joseph was "a righteous man" (1:19). He did not understand Mary's pregnancy, but after divine intervention, placed his trust in the words of the angel of the Lord. According to the Torah, he should have divorced her— and he would have been declared righteous by works—but following the angel's directive, he took her as his wife, trusting in God's reliability. Thus, like Abraham before him, Joseph is declared righteous by faith.

In a consumer culture, righteousness easily becomes a commodity to be earned or bought. For many people, going to church is like making a deposit in the bank. Sinning is like taking out some of the funds in one's heavenly savings account. In effect, this is salvation by works. No trust in God is required, since each person has his or her personal account.

Paul argues that righteousness is a gift offered by God to us. Abraham is the first person to have trusted God's reliability. Joseph is another. God makes the first move, and we respond in faith to God's offer of grace. God declares us righteous, to be in a healthy relationship with him. With each response we make, more grace—God's own life—is given to us, hopefully, evoking another response. According to Paul, this is how God draws us into righteousness.

Meditation: What was your first response to God's grace? Can you trace your growth in trust of God as you have kept responding to grace through faith?

Prayer: Father, you declared your servants Abraham and Joseph righteous through faith. Make us ever more aware of your daily offers of grace that we may grow in deeper trust of you, who raised Jesus Christ, your Son, from the dead. He lives and reigns with you and the Holy Spirit as one God, forever and ever. Amen.

Dreamer

(1) Matthew 1:16, 18–21, 24a

Scripture: ". . . Jacob [was] the father of Joseph the husband of Mary, of whom Jesus was born, who is called the Messiah" (Matthew 1:16).

Reflection: Most biblical scholars agree that Matthew's Joseph character is modeled on the Hebrew Bible (Old Testament) Joseph. The Joseph of Genesis has a father named Jacob; the Joseph of Matthew's Gospel is the son of Jacob. The Joseph of Genesis is the recipient of divine direction through dreams; the Joseph of Matthew's Gospel receives divine direction through the appearance of an angel of the Lord in his dreams. The Joseph of Genesis goes to Egypt; the Joseph of Matthew's Gospel takes Mary and Jesus to Egypt.

A dreamer comes to understand that he or she is part of something that is bigger than he or she. In the case of Joseph from Genesis, he comes to understand that his dreams got him to Egypt in order to save the world from famine. In the case of Joseph from Matthew's Gospel, he comes to understand that his dreams are a part of God's plan both to save Jesus and to save the world.

What we might not understand is that God works through our dreams to accomplish his will. A young man may marry the girl of his dreams, thinking that they are his dreams; later he discovers that his dreams were God's dreams, the Holy One's way of bringing children into the world, of fulfilling a mission of some kind, of being a living witness to the divine purpose.

The young woman meeting the man of her dreams thinks that she will fulfill her dreams by marrying him. However, her dreams may be God's dreams for her. She may be entrusted with more dreams that include adoption, teaching religion, hospice ministry, etc.

Our hopes, our dreams, mature gradually and come to fulfillment over the course of a lifetime. What the author of the Joseph story in the book of Genesis understood and what the author of Matthew's Gospel gleaned from Genesis is that God works through dreams. God's will or purpose unfolds only gradually in our lives. The dreams we have are most likely God's dreams for us. Bringing those dreams to reality means doing God's will.

Meditation: What do you think is God's dream for you? How has that understanding been revealed to you through your dreams?

Prayer: Ever-living God, you guided Joseph through his dreams to do your will. Fill us with the Holy Spirit to guide our dreams to do your will. Hear us through our Lord Jesus Christ, your Son, who lives and reigns with you and the Holy Spirit, one God, forever and ever. Amen.

Father

(2) Luke 2:41–51a

Scripture: [Jesus' mother said to him:] "Child, why have you treated us like this? Look, your father and I have been searching for you in great anxiety" (Luke 2:48).

Reflection: The second choice of a gospel passage for the Solemnity of St. Joseph is the second of two unique childhood stories about Jesus found in Luke's Gospel. The first is commonly known as the presentation in the temple, and the second is called the finding of the boy Jesus in the temple.

The story is set on the occasion of Passover, the Jewish commemoration of the death of the firstborn son in Egypt. As God's, Joseph's and Mary's firstborn son, Jesus will not return to Jerusalem until he prepares to mark his last Passover. Furthermore, Jesus is twelve years old; twelve is a sacred number, the product of three—the spiritual order—and four—the created order.

The twelve-year-old boy stays in Jerusalem, unknown to his parents, after the festival is over. When his parents fail to find him in their caravan, they turn around and go back to Jerusalem, searching for their son for three days, a holy time. They find him in the temple, sitting with the teachers, listening to them and asking them questions. This dialogue is a foreshadowing of the encounters that will occur between Jesus and the teachers throughout the rest of the gospel.

When Jesus' parents find him, his mother asks him why he has put them through the anxiety they have felt during their three days of searching for him. He replies with his own questions, "Why were you searching for me? Did you not know that I must be in my Father's house?" (2:49)

Luke stresses Jesus' conception by the Holy Spirit and the power of the Most High. The angel Gabriel tells Mary that the child she will conceive in her womb will be called "Son of God" (1:35). In today's passage, Jesus declares that he is in his Father's house, the temple. However, Luke also regards Joseph as Jesus' earthly father, who presents him to God in the temple and takes him to the temple on his twelfth birthday for Passover. Thus, "Father" refers both to God and to Joseph.

We address God as our Father often in prayer. Today, we honor Joseph as Jesus' father. While the role of fatherhood is always changing, today's pericope presents a few characteristics that are worthy of our reflection. First, as his earthly father, Joseph exposes Jesus to the traditions of his people. Passover is the most important feast on the Jewish calendar, and when he is old enough to understand it, Joseph takes Jesus to experience it. Modern fathers need to share religious feasts with their sons in addition to those associated with sports.

Second, Joseph trusts his son to be with the group of travelers. Trust remains an important virtue for fathers and sons to share even though it

Solemnity of St. Joseph, Husband of the Blessed Virgin Mary

may be violated often by twelve-year-old boys. However, they will never learn trust if they are never trusted.

Third, the innocent wisdom of a child is not to be dismissed. A son may say some amazing things. Fathers should ponder those truths, even if they do not understand them.

And fourth, obedience is to be insisted upon, but not abused. Jesus went home to Nazareth and was obedient to his father, while his mother treasured all these events in her heart. A son's obedience to his father provides the boundary for growth in both human and divine wisdom.

Meditation: What virtues does/did your father possess? How did they help you grow in both human and divine wisdom?

Prayer: God our Father, you entrusted the care of your only-begotten Son to St. Joseph. Help us to imitate his virtues that we may grow in knowledge of your ways. Guide us with the wisdom of the Holy Spirit, who lives and reigns with you, Father, and our Lord Jesus Christ, forever and ever. Amen.

❋ March 25
Solemnity of the Annunciation of the Lord

Immanuel

Isaiah 7:10–14; 8:10

Scripture: ". . . Isaiah said: '. . . [T]he Lord himself will give you [, King Ahaz,] a sign. Look, the young woman is with child and shall bear a son, and shall name him Immanuel'" (Isa 7:14).

Reflection: The biblical text for today's first reading on the Solemnity of the Annunciation of the Lord is chosen for two reasons. First, it is an annunciation by the prophet Isaiah. Second, this is the fulfillment quotation used by the author of Matthew's Gospel (1:23) after Joseph is instructed to name Mary's son Jesus. It is also alluded to in Luke's narrative of the annunciation (1:27).

In context, the reader needs to know that King Ahaz of Judah is attacked by an alliance of other kings, including the King of Israel. The small southern kingdom of Judah was not going to be able to withstand the coalition of enemies. However, the LORD promises Ahaz that the Davidic dynasty will continue despite the alliance. The LORD invites King Ahaz to ask for a sign, any sign as "deep as Sheol or high as heaven" (7:11) that the prophetic word would be fulfilled. Ahaz, however, refuses because he is seeking military help from Assyria.

So, the prophet Isaiah announces that the sign will be "the young woman . . . with child [who] shall bear a son, and shall name him Immanuel" (7:14). What Isaiah announces is that King Ahaz's wife will give him an heir so that the Davidic line will continue. In due time, Ahaz's son, Hezekiah, was born, and Assyria came to conquer Israel and make Judah a vassal.

Solemnity of the Annunciation of the Lord

The name Isaiah gives to the new king is the second in a series of names, each having a specific prophetic meaning. The birth of Ahaz's son, Hezekiah, serves as the Lord's sign of his presence with the king of Judah. The name means "God is with us" (8:10).

After Judah fell to the Babylonians in 587 BC and the Davidic monarchy came to an end, the name "Immanuel" was used in popular messianic expectation of a new king who, like David, would drive out the Roman occupation forces of Palestine and restore self-rule to the country once again. However, this never happened. So, in due time, the author of Matthew's Gospel came to understand that Jesus was the new king who came to establish a kingdom that was not of this world. Thus, Matthew understands Jesus' birth as fulfilling Isaiah's promise of a sign to Ahaz.

Celebrating the Solemnity of the Annunciation of the Lord, which is never marked on a Sunday, gives us the opportunity to reflect upon our names as signs. If Immanuel is a sign of God's presence to King Ahaz, in what capacity does our name serve as a sign of God's presence to ourselves and others? For example, "Mark" means "brave," and can serve as a sign of God's bravery in the face of oppression. "David" and "Mary" mean "beloved," referring to the relationship God established with both of them. "Jesus" means "Yahweh is salvation," indicating that God was saving his people in the person of Jesus. Get a biblical dictionary or go online and find the meaning of your name and how it is a sign of God's presence to you and to others.

Meditation: What does your name mean? How is it a sign of God's presence to you and others?

Prayer: Ever-living God, you bestow signs of your presence upon your people to awaken them to your power to save. As we celebrate the Solemnity of the Annunciation of your Son, make us grateful for the salvation you bestowed on us through him who is named Jesus Christ. He lives and reigns with you and the Holy Spirit, one God, forever and ever. Amen.

God's Will

Hebrews 10:4–10

Scripture: ". . . [W]hen Christ came into the world, he said, 'See, God, I have come to do your will, O God' (in the scroll of the book it is written of me)" (Heb 10:5, 7).

Reflection: The author of Hebrews, a sermon illustrating the high priesthood of Jesus Christ, contrasts the offering of animal sacrifices with Christ's obedient offering of himself to God. Using Psalm 40:6-8, which serves as today's Responsorial Psalm, the author declares that God did not desire nor take pleasure in sacrifices and offerings. What God desires, according to Hebrews, is obedience to his will. Thus, Christ "abolishes the first in order to establish the second" covenant (10:9). Hebrews continues, "It is by God's will that we have been sanctified through the offering of the body of Jesus Christ once for all" (10:10). The obedience of Jesus to God all the way to his death on the cross is what God desires of us. In other words, Jesus is a model of faithfulness for us.

This passage from Hebrews is chosen as the second reading on the Solemnity of the Annunciation of the Lord because it contains the announcement of God's will and it focuses on the result of Jesus doing that will, namely, the sanctification of all people through his death and resurrection. Because animals are not rational, they could not do God's will; they became sacrifices offered to God by humans, but God took no pleasure in burnt offerings that could not take away sins. Because Jesus, a human being, was rational, he could do God's will; he offered himself as a sacrifice to God, and God not only took pleasure in his self-offering, but God made that self-offering the means whereby sins were removed once for all.

All who follow Jesus walk in his footsteps of faithfulness; they do God's will, which must be discerned through reading Scripture, through dialogue with others, through the help of a spiritual director. It is much easier to do our own wills. We decide our lifestyle, we choose our career, what place we live, what house we buy, etc. Faithfulness to God, however, often calls us to renounce our desires and offer ourselves in obedience to doing God's will. In a culture saturated with ego, it is often hard to hear God's announcements to us.

Solemnity of the Annunciation of the Lord

Meditation: What is God's will for you? Have you been obediently faithful?

Prayer: O God, sacrifices and offerings you have not desired, but a body you have prepared for us so that we might do your will. Guide our discernment through the power of the Holy Spirit, and keep us faithful to the example of your Son, Jesus Christ, who lives and reigns with you and the Holy Spirit, one God, forever and ever. Amen.

Announcement

Luke 1:26-38

Scripture: "The angel [Gabriel] said to [Mary], 'Do not be afraid, Mary, for you have found favor with God. And now, you will conceive in your womb and bear a son, and you will name him Jesus'" (Luke 1:30-31).

Reflection: This gospel passage is read multiple times during the liturgical year. It is most appropriate, however, on the Solemnity of the Annunciation of the Lord—which is never celebrated on a Sunday—because it contains the angel Gabriel's announcement of the conception and birth of Jesus, who is often referred to as "Lord" by the author of Luke's Gospel.

"In the sixth month" of Elizabeth's pregnancy "the angel Gabriel was sent by God to a town in Galilee called Nazareth, to a virgin engaged to a man whose name was Joseph of the house of David. The Virgin's name was Mary" (1:26-27). Luke understands Isaiah's words to King Ahaz about the LORD giving Ahaz a sign—namely, that the young woman or virgin is with child and shall bear a son—to be fulfilled by Gabriel's words to Mary: "Do not be afraid, Mary, for you have found favor with God. And now, you will conceive in your womb and bear a son, and you will name him Jesus" (1:30-31).

Mary is God's favored one, chosen for a special role. Gabriel explains that the child she will conceive "will be great, and will be called the Son of the Most High, and the Lord God will give to him the throne of his ancestor David" (1:32). Luke makes several important points with Gabriel's words to Mary. First, Isaiah's "Immanuel"—God with us—will occur in Mary's womb. Second, the everlasting covenant promised to David and his descendants becomes a kingdom having no end.

Echoing the "Immanuel" name, Luke narrates Gabriel's answer to Mary's question about how a virgin can conceive: "The Holy Spirit will come upon you, and the power of the Most High will overshadow you; therefore the child to be born will be holy; he will be called Son of God" (1:35). In other words, Luke introduces one of his favorite themes here. That theme is that Jesus is a Spirit child. As such, he is filled with the Holy Spirit from his conception, and he will be "led by the Spirit" (4:1) throughout the rest of the gospel.

Luke imagines Mary as a new ark of the covenant. In the first ark, the tablets of the Law represented the presence of God with his people. That ark was often overshadowed by a cloud, which protected the Israelites from harm and from the brightness of God's holiness. With her divine conception of God's Son, Mary is a new ark, protected by God from harm and given the overwhelming grace of the Holy One's favor.

Mary is given the sign that the reader already knows: ". . . Elizabeth in her old age has . . . conceived a son; and this is the sixth month for her who was said to be barren" (1:36). Luke, following in the footsteps of Isaiah, likes to give signs that verify the angel's words. Isaiah, Luke's favorite prophet, often gives signs that indicate that God will fulfill the words he inspires his prophet to speak to his people.

Once she understands the sign that indicates that "nothing will be impossible with God" (1:37), Mary accepts Gabriel's annunciation, declaring, "Here am I, the servant of the Lord; let it be with me according to your word" (1:38). Luke quickly brings to an end this annunciation that parallels the one of Gabriel announcing to Zechariah that his wife Elizabeth will conceive in her old age and give birth to John the Baptist (1:5–25). Gabriel leaves the gospel never to reappear.

We receive announcements all the time. Most of our wedding announcements, graduation announcements, birth announcements, etc. come through ground mail or e-mail. Modern angels visit us in modern ways and deliver God's words to us. A few words from a homily may spark our thoughts about something we need to do for our spiritual lives. A newspaper article may get us to write that check as a donation to a worthy cause that we have been putting off for a few weeks. An Internet story may urge us to seek more information about a religious topic about which we have

Solemnity of the Annunciation of the Lord

always wondered. God sends announcements to us in many ways; we, like Mary, must be ready to receive them.

Meditation: What recent announcement have you received from God? What action did it spark you to take?

Prayer: Most High God, you sent your angel Gabriel to Mary of Nazareth to announce the conception and birth of your Son. Help us to hear your word in the Scriptures, in preachers and teachers, and in each other. Grant us the favor to respond through our Lord Jesus Christ, who lives and reigns with you and the Holy Spirit, one God, forever and ever. Amen.

✤ April 25
Feast of St. Mark, Evangelist

Love

1 Peter 5:5b–14

Scripture: "Your sister church in Babylon, chosen together with you, sends you greetings; and so does my son Mark" (1 Pet 5:13).

Reflection: The first biblical passage assigned for the Feast of St. Mark is the last ten verses of the first letter of Peter, written at the end of the first century or early in the second century AD to those Christians, "brothers and sisters in all the world . . . undergoing . . . suffering" (5:9), that is, undergoing persecution in Roman provinces. The letter is written "to encourage" the readers and "to testify that this [suffering] is the true grace of God" (5:12) in which they should stand fast. Believing in an imminent return of Christ, the author exhorts his readers to endure their suffering for a short time because "the God of all grace, who has called [them] to his eternal glory in Christ, will himself restore, support, strengthen, and establish [them]" (5:10).

Biblical scholars do not think that the historical Peter—who was martyred between 64 and 68 AD—wrote this letter, but a high ranking church official, possibly living in Rome—identified as the "sister church in Babylon" (5:13)—wrote it in Peter's name to establish his authority to address Christians on certain issues. The writer's secretary is named Silvanus, a faithful brother or fellow believer.

Today's passage contains the last verses of the household duties of elders, more specifically, the humility they need in dealing with one another, especially in time of anxiety. The author tells them to discipline themselves, to keep alert. "Like a roaring lion [the] adversary, the devil, prowls around,

Feast of St. Mark, Evangelist

looking for someone to devour" (5:8). A bit of irony may be present in this verse for those who know that Mark's Gospel is represented in popular iconography by a winged lion. Of course this is not the only irony contained in this feast; see the entry on Mark 16:15–20 below.

The major reason this passage is chosen for the Feast of St. Mark is because it mentions the name "Mark" (5:13). According to an unreliable tradition, Mark, which means "brave," is mentioned as an associate of Peter in Rome. However, because the name Mark was as common a Roman name in the first and second century as John is today, whoever is being referred to in 1 Peter is most likely not the same person who wrote Mark's Gospel.

The instruction to "greet one another with a kiss of love" (5:14) reminds the readers that they are identified by their "genuine mutual love" (1:22) as a household or family. Earlier in the letter, readers are commanded, "Love the family of believers" (2:17), and "[M]aintain constant love for one another, for love covers a multitude of sins" (4:8). The refrain of Peter Scholtes' hymn, "They'll Know We Are Christians," captures this sentiment: "And they'll know we are Christians by our love, by our love, Yes they'll know we are Christians by our love."

The love that 1 Peter writes about is not the sappy sentimentality or the emotional-laden feeling or the general "I love everything" that the word "love" carries with it today. 1 Peter understands love as the sacrifice of self for the good of others. In other words, mutual love indicates that others come first, before the self. Such sacrificial love imitates Jesus, who loved us all the way to the cross.

Meditation: Where do you find genuine sacrificial love in your Christian community?

Prayer: Almighty God, you loved the world so much that you sent your only Son to save it. Jesus taught and lived sacrificial love, opening his arms on the cross. Grant that we may imitate his example and so share in the promise of Mark's Gospel. We ask this through the same Christ our Lord. Amen.

Irony

Mark 16:15–20

Scripture: [Jesus said to the Eleven,] "Go into all the world and proclaim the good news to the whole creation" (Mark 16:15).

Reflection: If one opens his or her Bible to Mark's Gospel, chapter 16, he or she will quickly notice that it has three endings. Biblical scholars have determined that the original ending is 16:8. Another verse is added to 16:8 to form the shorter ending of Mark. And verses 9 through 20 form the longer ending of Mark. All three endings are canonical.

The irony of the Feast of St. Mark is that whoever wrote the rest of the gospel did not write the passage assigned to be read today. The pericope for today is a part of the longer ending of Mark which differs in style and emphasis from the rest of the gospel. The longer ending seems to be a compilation of the endings of Matthew's Gospel, Luke's Gospel and the Acts of the Apostles, and John's Gospel, echoing the Emmaus story, the great commissioning, the ascension, and more. It also contradicts Jesus' refusal to give signs in Mark's Gospel by portraying him now giving signs to those who believe.

Besides the irony found in the gospel reading, irony is present in celebrating this feast
of a gospel writer, whoever he was, about whom we know absolutely nothing. We know that someone had to write Mark's Gospel, but the author is forever lost in human history, since this gospel did not have a name until the second century.

Throughout the Bible, we find God's irony, and maybe that is what we are celebrating on this feast of St. Mark. God's irony is found throughout biblical literature. God calls Abraham and Sarah to be the parents of a multitude of people, except that Sarah is barren. God calls Moses to lead his people out of slavery to freedom, except that Moses has a speech impediment. God calls Peter to be the closest of Jesus' companions, except that Peter denies knowing Jesus three times—in every gospel.

The truth of this feast might be found in the irony of our own lives. If we gaze deeply into our own lives, we might find God's irony written there with big letters. Sometimes, God's irony comes through illness of any kind. The very illness that weakens us also strengthens our faith and our

Feast of St. Mark, Evangelist

commitment to God. At other times, God's irony comes financially. How many times have we heard people tell us that the more we give away, the more it comes back to us? And God's irony may come through our personal relationships. The person we can fight with the best is often the person we love the most.

See, God's truth can shine through the irony of our lives. As we celebrate this feast we do well to reflect upon God's irony in our lives and the truth it teaches us. Then, we will have connected ourselves to the irony found in the Bible and the irony inherent in this feast of St. Mark.

Meditation: What irony in your life reveals God at work there?

Prayer: Almighty God, you entrusted the proclamation of the good news of your Son to Mark, your evangelist. Help us recognize your work in the irony of our lives, that we may proclaim to the whole creation that Jesus is Lord to your glory. We ask this through Christ, who lives and reigns with you and the Holy Spirit, one God, forever and ever. Amen.

�֎ May 1
Optional Memorial of St. Joseph the Worker

Carpenter's Son

Matthew 13:54–58

Scripture: "[Jesus] came to his hometown and began to teach the people in their synagogue, so that they were astounded and said, 'Where did this man get this wisdom and these deeds of power? Is not this the carpenter's son? Is not his mother called Mary? And are not his brothers James and Joseph and Simon and Judas?'" (Matt 13:54–55)

Reflection: Matthew's account of Jesus' rejection in Nazareth comes from Mark's Gospel (6:1–6). Matthew, as he often does, shortens and alters material he borrows from Mark. For example, in Mark's Gospel those who hear Jesus in the synagogue ask, "Is not this the carpenter, the son of Mary . . . ?" (6:3) To refer to a man as the son of his mother is a slur; in Judaism a man is known as the son of his father. Matthew rewrites the account he finds in Mark's Gospel to remove the slur. Jesus is referred to as the "carpenter's son," whose "mother [is] called Mary" (13:55).

Thus, Matthew transfers Mark's description of Jesus as a carpenter to Joseph. The Greek word used by both Mark and Matthew means "artisan" and might better be translated as "craftsman" or "builder." It is broader in meaning that our usual understanding of carpenter as one who works with wood.

In modifying Mark's story, Matthew declares that Jesus is much more than a craftsman. However, his father, Joseph, was a carpenter, according to Matthew. Thus, we are given today's optional memorial of St. Joseph the Worker and an opportunity to reflect on work in a culture that seems to despise it or find any way possible to avoid it.

Optional Memorial of St. Joseph the Worker

Work is the way we make a living, no matter if it is manual labor as a stone mason, a carpenter, a construction employee or office labor as a receptionist, a secretary, or an accountant. According to the U.S. Bishops' pastoral letter, "Economic Justice for All: Catholic Social Teaching and the U.S. Economy," ". . . [I]t is primarily through their daily labor that people make their most important contributions to economic justice" (96).

According to the bishops: "All work has a threefold moral significance. First, it is the principal way that people exercise the distinctive human capacity for self-expression and self-realization. Second, it is the ordinary way for human beings to fulfill their material needs. Finally, work enables people to contribute to the well-being of the larger community" (97).

Each of these three points is worthy of our reflection. Work is for oneself; people express who they are through the careers they choose. The work they do brings people to self-realization; that is, it assists in the growth and development of each person.

However, work is not just for oneself. Yes, it is the ordinary means for meeting individual material needs and for financial security. However, it also contributes to the common good of one's family, one's city, one's nation. And in many cases, a person's work contributes to the common good of the whole world.

In celebrating the memorial of St. Joseph the Worker, we are focusing on the dignity of human work and the moral significance of it. As a carpenter, craftsman, or builder, St. Joseph expressed himself in what he made. His skill enabled him to support his wife and foster child. And his work contributed to the common good of Nazareth, Palestine, and the Roman world of the first century AD.

Meditation: How is your work an expression of who you are? How does your work contribute to the larger community?

Prayer: Creator God, in the beginning you made the heavens and the earth and all they contain. You declared your work to be a holy. Sanctify us through the work we do, and, through the intercession of St. Joseph, bring us to the fullness of life you promise. We ask this through our Lord Jesus Christ, your Son, who lives and reigns with you and the Holy Spirit, one God, forever and ever. Amen.

✣ May 3
Feast of Sts. Philip and James, Apostles

Tradition

1 Corinthians 15:1–8

Scripture: Brothers and sisters, ". . . I [, Paul,] handed on to you as of first importance what I in turn had received: that Christ died for our sins in accordance with the scriptures, and that he was buried, and that he was raised on the third day in accordance with the scriptures, and that he appeared to Cephas, then to the twelve" (1 Cor 15:1–5).

Reflection: The first biblical passage assigned to the Feast of Sts. Philip and James comes from chapter 15 of Paul's first letter to the Corinthians. The first eleven verses, which serve as a summary of the transmission of Christian preaching and teaching, introduce the topic of the chapter: resurrection. Today's passage consists of only the first eight verses of the introductory material.

The pattern of preaching and teaching in Pauline churches consists of four steps: (1) Christ died. (2) Christ was buried. (3) Christ was raised. (4) Christ appeared.

"Christ died for our sins in accordance with the scriptures" (15:3), Paul writes to the Corinthians. He understands Jesus' death through the lens of Isaiah 53:5: The suffering servant "was wounded for our transgression, crushed for our iniquities; upon him was the punishment that made us whole, and by his bruises we are healed."

To guarantee the reality of Jesus' death, he must be buried. However, using the lens of Hosea 6:2 ("After two days [the LORD] will revive us; on the third day he will raise us up, that we may live before him."), Paul declares that God raised Jesus from the dead. And to prove that he had

Feast of Sts. Philip and James, Apostles

been raised by God Christ appeared or showed himself to Peter (Cephas), the twelve, and more than 500 others, "most of whom are still alive" (15:6) and available for questioning. "Then," according to Paul—and the reason this pericope is chosen for this feast—"he appeared to James, then to all the apostles" (15:7).

Paul understands that God was at work in these events, just as God is at work today in the events of our lives. The pattern of preaching and teaching remains, and we can see it in our daily lives if we spend some time reflecting upon it. Because the events Paul names are not the most pleasant, we have a tendency to presume that God is not there.

For example, God is at work in death. Christ died. Our relatives and friends have died. One day we, too, will die. It is not that God wills death, but that it is a natural conclusion to life. When we have fulfilled our purpose, we will die.

And we will be buried. Christ was buried. Today, we may be cremated and have our ashes buried. No matter whether we opt for bodily interment or cremains interment, the fact of our death will be demonstrated through some form of burial.

Christ was raised. And we await the same fate. God has promised that those who remain faithful will be raised to new life with Christ. Through death, we pass over to new life. Death changes life; it does not end it. In the Nicene Creed each person declares, "I look forward to the resurrection of the dead and the life of the world to come."

Christ appeared. And we hope to appear with him one day. When Christ returns in glory, the last judgment will come. According to the *Catechism of the Catholic Church*, "The Last Judgment will reveal even to its furthest consequences the good each person has done or failed to do during his [or her] earthly life" (1039).

In celebrating the feast of Sts. Philip and James, we come to realize that the tradition that Paul handed on to the Corinthians in the middle of the first century AD is the same tradition that has been handed on to us: (1) Christ died. (2) Christ was buried. (3) Christ was raised. (4) Christ appeared. In it we continue to stand.

Meditation: How do you find the pattern of preaching and teaching in Pauline churches present in your life?

Prayer: Lord of heaven and earth, you reveal your glory through the death, burial, resurrection, and appearances of your Son, Jesus Christ. As we embrace this teaching handed on to us, trace in us the same pattern that we may one day share in the fullness of your Trinitarian life. You are one God—Father, Son, and Holy Spirit—forever and ever. Amen.

God's Works

John 14:6–14

Scripture: "Philip said to [Jesus], 'Lord, show us the Father, and we will be satisfied.' Jesus said to him, 'Have I been with you all this time, Philip, and you still do not know me? Whoever has seen me has seen the Father'" (John 14:9).

Reflection: The gospel assigned to the Feast of Sts. Philip and James comes from the four-chapter insert between 13:38 and 18:1 of John's Gospel, which, except for very little dialogue, features Jesus giving discourse after discourse. The first five verses of the insert are omitted; in them Jesus explains that he is going away to prepare a place for his disciples, and they know the place where he is going. This prompts Jesus to declare: "I am the way, and the truth, and the life. No one comes to the Father except through me" (14:6). Then, Jesus adds: "If you know me, you will know my Father also. From now on you do know him and have seen him" (14:7).

This causes Philip to say, "Lord, show us the Father, and we will be satisfied" (14:8), and Jesus to ask: "Have I been with you all this time, Philip, and you still do not know me? Whoever has seen me has seen the Father" (14:9).

First, in Judaism everyone knew that the way to God was adherence to the Torah. So, when the Johannine Jesus declares that he is the way, the truth, and the life, he is replacing the function of the Law. Throughout John's Gospel, Jesus is portrayed as one who replaces the Law, Jewish feasts, and more. He is not just a guide to the Father; Jesus is the source of the Father's life and truth.

Second, in John's Gospel Jesus is the incarnate presence of God; he is God in human flesh. Jesus is the visual image of the invisible God; he is the visible icon of the invisible Father. Because he is in the Father and the Father is in him, whoever sees Jesus sees the Father. Even Jesus' audible words are those of the inaudible Father. Jesus is the revelation of the Father.

Third, because Jesus is in the Father and the Father is in him, those who believe in Jesus abide in him and become vehicles for the Father's works. Once Jesus returns to the Father through his death and resurrection, those who live in him can ask anything in his name, and he will do it.

It is this third point that ties this passage to the Feast of Sts. Philip and James. Apostles, those who were sent into the world by the Son, are vehicles for the Father's ongoing works through their union with Jesus, who promises them divine assistance through the presence of an Advocate, the Spirit of truth.

We have been incorporated—embodied—into Christ through baptism. As members of his body, we are the means for the Father to continue his work. We are filled with the Father's life, and our works, inspired by the Spirit, are the works of God, if we abide in Jesus. Because we tend to distinguish ourselves from Jesus, we end up separating ourselves from him. And the result is that we do our own works instead of the Father's works. It is only by careful discernment of the promptings of the Spirit that we can know what God's will is and then proceed to do it.

Meditation: In what specific ways have you been a vehicle for God's work?

Prayer: Father of our Lord Jesus Christ, you gave Philip and James as apostles to your Son, who sent them into the world to proclaim your marvelous works. Through the Holy Spirit, help us to know your will for our lives and give us the courage to accomplish it. We ask this through the same Jesus Christ, who lives and reigns with you and the Holy Spirit, one God, forever and ever. Amen.

✥ May 14
Feast of St. Matthias, Apostle

Matthias

Acts 1:15–17, 20–26

Scripture: The believers "cast lots" for Joseph called Barsabbas and Matthias, "and the lot fell on Matthias; and he was added to the eleven apostles" (Acts 1:26).

Reflection: In Luke's Gospel, the first of a two-volume work—the second volume is the Acts of the Apostles—Jesus chooses twelve men (Luke 6:14–16). After Jesus' death and resurrection, Peter leads the assembly of believers in choosing a twelfth man to replace Judas, who, in verses omitted from today's passage, fell headlong into a field, burst open in the middle, and all his bowels gushed out (1:18). After two men were nominated, the believers prayed and then cast lots for the position. Matthias, who is never named again, was the winner.

Several important points present themselves for our reflection on this passage from the Acts of the Apostles. First, this is the first speech Peter gives after the Ascension of Jesus into heaven. Luke, the author of this speech, carefully interprets what happened to Judas based on Psalm 69:25: "May their camp be a desolation; let no one live in their tents" and Psalm 109:8: "May his days be few; may another seize his position."

Second, whoever is chosen to fill the vacancy left by Judas must be "one of the men who had accompanied [the believers] all the time that the Lord Jesus went in and out among [them], beginning from the baptism of John until the day when he was taken up from [them]—one of these must become a witness with [them] to his resurrection" (Acts 1:21–22). To be witness is to be a martyr, one who undergoes suffering and death—with hope of resurrection—in imitation of Jesus. This Lukan theme is best presented in Jesus' innocent death in Luke's Gospel and Stephen's innocent death in the Acts of the Apostles (see December 26 below).

Third, Peter leads the apostles in doing what Jesus had done. Throughout Luke and Acts, whatever Jesus does in Luke's Gospel, the apostles—particularly Peter and Paul—do in the Acts. Jesus heals a cripple; Peter and Paul each heal a cripple. Jesus raises the dead; both Peter and Paul raise someone from the dead. Jesus chose twelve men; the apostles choose a twelfth man to replace Judas. Later in the Acts they will also choose seven men to assist in the daily distribution of food.

The twelve needs to be reconstituted in order to prepare for Pentecost, which is the next event narrated in the Acts of the Apostles. Just as the Holy Spirit launched the gospel—with Mary, Elizabeth, Zechariah, and Jesus filled with him—so does the Holy Spirit launch the Acts of the Apostles. Just as the Holy Spirit guides the events in Luke's Gospel, so does the Holy Spirit guide the events of the Acts of the Apostles.

The Twelve apostles parallel the twelve tribes of Israel. Just like God chose twelve tribes and united them under King David, so Jesus chose twelve men and united them to him. Matthias' sole purpose is to be apostle number twelve, since he is never mentioned again in the Acts of the Apostles or, for that matter, in the New Testament.

He fulfilled his purpose. He was entrusted with the good news that Christ had died, Christ had been raised, Christ had ascended, Christ had given the gift of the Spirit, and Christ will come again in glory. Like all the apostles of the past, we did not choose to be sent as messengers of the gospel. We have been chosen and sent by others who, like Peter and the believers, called Matthias for the same purpose.

Meditation: What is your purpose as an apostle of Jesus Christ? To whom have you been sent? To where have you been sent?

Prayer: Holy Spirit, breathe new life in the apostles of your Church, and make us effective proclaimers of the message of the gospel of Jesus Christ. May we imitate the apostle Matthias, and bring glory to the Father and the Son, who live and reign with you as one God, forever and ever. Amen.

Chosen

John 15:9–17

Scripture: Jesus said to his disciples: "You did not choose me but I chose you. And I appointed you to go and bear fruit, fruit that will last, so that the Father will give you whatever you ask him in my name" (John 15:16).

Reflection: The gospel assigned to the Feast of St. Matthias comes from the four-chapter insert between 13:38 and 18:1 of John's Gospel, which, except for very little dialogue, features Jesus giving one discourse after another. Today's verses conclude the vine and branches speech in which Jesus replaces Israel as the true vine.

The Johannine theology is that Jesus is the incarnate presence of God on earth. Jesus is in the Father, and the Father is in Jesus. By keeping the commandment of love, Jesus' disciples abide in his love, and, because he abides in the Father's love, they abide in God's love. Being one with God through Jesus completes the disciples' joy.

Furthermore, the love that God and Jesus share—and the love into which the disciples are invited—is sacrificial love; a person puts others ahead of himself or herself to the point of being willing to lay down his or her life for his or her friends. Jesus names his disciples friends, because he has revealed to them the love of the Father and he will lay down his life for them.

This passage is presented on the Feast of St. Matthias because it echoes the pericope from the Acts of the Apostles, especially with Jesus' declaration, "You did not choose me but I chose you" (15:16). Matthias did not choose to be an apostle; he was chosen by Jesus after prayer and casting lots, under the leadership of Peter and the guidance of the Advocate or Holy Spirit.

Abiding in Jesus means to obey Jesus' commandment to love sacrificially. To abide means to remain stable. Like branches on the vine abide on the vine, those who abide in Jesus remain connected to the Father, the source of all life. Those who remain in Jesus discover complete joy and bear fruit abundantly.

Meditation: In what specific ways do you abide in Jesus? How is sacrificial love required of each of those specific ways?

Feast of St. Matthias, Apostle

Prayer: Heavenly Father, through your Son, you have chosen us to bear fruit. Draw us deeper into your life, and make our joy complete. We ask this through our Lord Jesus Christ, who abides with you and the Holy Spirit, one God, forever and ever. Amen.

✠ May 31
Feast of the Visitation of the Blessed Virgin Mary

(1) God's Presence

Zephaniah 3:14–18a

Scripture: "The king of Israel, the LORD is in your midst; you shall fear disaster no more" (Zeph 3:15bc).

Reflection: The passage from the prophet Zephaniah presented as the first option for a first reading on the Feast of the Visitation of the Blessed Virgin Mary does not fit with the rest of the doom and gloom of the prophetic book. Therefore, many biblical scholars consider today's pericope a part of a longer addition to the book meant to offer hope of Jerusalem's restoration to the Jewish exiles after 587 BC. Zechariah sees "the remnant of Israel" (3:13) returning from Babylonian captivity.

This is why he exhorts poetically, "Sing aloud, O daughter Zion; shout, O Israel! Rejoice and exult with all your heart, O daughter Jerusalem!" (3:14). The exiles returning to Jerusalem from Babylon should exult because, in Zechariah's words, "The LORD has taken away the judgments against [them], he has turned away [their] enemies" (3:15). The holy city Jerusalem, which was forsaken by the king and God now can boast that the king of Israel, the LORD, is in her midst and no further disaster will befall her. Indeed, God the warrior leads his people to victory, rejoicing over them with gladness, renewing them in his love, and signing loudly as on a festival.

This passage is presented as an optional first reading on the Feast of the Visitation of the Blessed Virgin Mary to highlight God's presence in the womb of Mary, daughter Zion, daughter Jerusalem, as she visits her relative, Elizabeth. The passage also serves to highlight the two beatitudes spoken by

Feast of the Visitation of the Blessed Virgin Mary

Elizabeth and the song sung by Mary. Mary's visit with Elizabeth erupts with gladness, love, and loud singing because God is visiting his people.

Modern people have a tendency to relegate God's presence to a building, forgetting that the world is filled with the Divine. The water of a flowing stream or raging river serves as a reminder of the Holy One's grace or gift of himself. The strength we have to pray is itself a manifestation of the LORD God's salvation. A cross or statue can be a reminder that the Holy One of Israel is in our midst.

Meditation: Where do you discover God's presence?

Prayer: We give thanks to you, O LORD God, and we call upon your name as we praise you for all your glorious works throughout the whole earth. Give us a greater awareness of your presence in our midst that we may never cease to shout aloud and sing to you, Father, Son, and Holy Spirit, one God, forever and ever. Amen.

(2) Community

Romans 12:9–16

Scripture: "Rejoice in hope, be patient in suffering, persevere in prayer" (Rom 12:12).

Reflection: The second option for a first reading for the Feast of the Visitation of the Blessed Virgin Mary is taken from Paul's letter to the Romans. It follows a series of moral exhortations, especially one of Paul's favorite metaphors about "we, who are many, are one body in Christ, and individually we are members one of another" (12:5). Genuine love, especially that which outdoes another in showing honor, should flow through the community that identifies itself as the one body in Christ. In other words, members do not play community, like one would play house as a child; they live community to the degree that they put each other ahead of each other, never lagging in zeal, always ardent in spirit and serving the Lord.

Paul summarizes a theme upon which he had elaborated earlier in the letter: "Rejoice in hope, be patient in suffering, persevere in prayer"

(12:12). Hope, for Paul, is "sharing the glory of God" (5:2), just like Christ Jesus already shares it through his resurrection from the dead. With that kind of hope members in Christ's body can suffer patiently; they can "boast in [their] sufferings, knowing that suffering produces endurance, and endurance produces character, and character produces hope" (5:3–4). Hope does not disappoint "because God's love has been poured into [their] hearts through the Holy Spirit that has been given to [them]" (5:5). Believers can even bless those who persecute them instead of cursing them. These community practices enable the members to "live in harmony with one another" (12:16).

The reason this short passage is chosen for the Feast of the Visitation of the Blessed Virgin Mary is found in these words of exhortation: "Rejoice with those who rejoice, weep with those who weep" (12:15). Rejoicing is what Elizabeth does when Mary visits her. Rejoicing is what Mary does when she breaks into song about God's blessings.

In a personalized culture, the individual always comes first, and the community is seldom considered. In a biblical culture, the community always comes first, and the individual is seldom considered. That is why Paul always focuses on the good of the whole first. Everything he writes about individual behavior is governed by the good of the community. The Feast of the Visitation of the Blessed Virgin Mary gives us the opportunity to reflect upon our role in the community, especially our genuine love, showing honor, being zealous, rejoicing in hope, being patient in suffering, persevering in prayer. When the community comes first, the needs of others are easily recognized, and hospitality is quickly extended to strangers.

Meditation: Identify three specific ways that you put the good of the community ahead of your own individual desires?

Prayer: We magnify you, O Lord, and our spirits rejoice in you, O God our Savior. We praise you, Mighty One, for all the great things you have done for us, especially the gift of salvation in the person of your Son. As we celebrate the visitation of the Blessed Virgin Mary to Elizabeth, make us so aware of your mercy that we deepen our love for each other. Through our Lord Jesus Christ, who lives and reigns with you and the Holy Spirit, one God, forever and ever. Amen.

Feast of the Visitation of the Blessed Virgin Mary

Visit

Luke 1:39–56

Scripture: "In those days Mary set out and went with haste to a Judean town in the hill country, where she entered the house of Zechariah and greeted Elizabeth" (Luke 1:39–40).

Reflection: Today's feast of the Visitation of the Blessed Virgin Mary is a biblical feast, meaning that it comes directly from Luke's Gospel. Immediately after entertaining the angel Gabriel and expressing her willingness to bear the Son of God, Mary leaves Nazareth and heads to the hill country to the home of Zechariah and Elizabeth, who in her old age has conceived a child according to Gabriel's words. Mary greets Elizabeth, her child stirs in her womb, and she declares Mary to be blessed among women. In response, Mary sings a hymn, which we know as the Magnificat.

Luke's narrative of Mary's visit to Elizabeth is a part of the author's unique two-chapter introduction to his "orderly account" (1:3) or gospel. After narrating the annunciation of John the Baptist's birth to Zechariah (and Elizabeth) by Gabriel, Luke narrates the annunciation of Jesus' birth to Mary (and Joseph) by Gabriel. The visitation serves to tie together the two annunciations, to bring together John and Jesus, and to specify the roles that each will play in the yet-to-be-unfolded "orderly account."

Mary's hymn is modeled upon Hannah's in 1 Samuel 2:1–10. It illustrates the biblical theme that God is in charge of everything. Mary praises God for his mercy "for those who fear him" which stretches "from generation to generation" (1:50). Then, the hymn presents the outline for the rest of the gospel. Through the ministry of Jesus, God will pull down the mighty from their thrones and exalt the lowly; he will feed the hungry and send away the rich; and he will save the people of Israel.

In the context of today's feast, we do well to reflect upon the concept of visitation. All of us have both been visited and been visitors. Family members and friends have come to visit us at home, in the hospital, at work. We have visited family members and friends in their homes, in the hospital, and at work.

Because God is omnipresent, the Holy One is always visiting his people. Often, however, our presuppositions as to where and when God will visit get in the way of recognizing the many and various appearances of God. Luke narrates that God visits in the hill country, in the Virgin's womb, in a sterile womb. God visits through prayer, a walk in the garden, a goose-bump raising breeze, etc. God's visits, like Mary's, are unannounced; often, they interrupt our day. But they bring new life to us; they cause new life to stir within us, like Elizabeth's child leaping in her womb. Once we are aware of the visitation, all we can do is praise God, like Mary did, for his unexpected surprise.

Meditation: When have you most recently been visited by God?

Prayer: Ever-present God, you visited Mary through the angel Gabriel, and Mary visited Elizabeth, causing John to leap for joy in her womb. Through the Holy Spirit, grant us the grace to recognize the visitations you make in our lives, that we may welcome your Son, our Lord Jesus Christ, with joy and praise you forever and ever. Amen.

✠ Friday after the Second Sunday after Pentecost
Solemnity of the Most Sacred Heart of Jesus

CYCLE A

Chosen

Deuteronomy 7:6–11

Scripture: "Moses convened all Israel, and said to them: . . . [Y]ou are a people holy to the LORD your God; the LORD your God has chosen you out of all the people on earth to be his people, his treasured possession" (Deut 5:1a; 7:6).

Reflection: Today's first reading from the Book of Deuteronomy, which portrays Moses giving an extended speech to the Israelites before they cross the Jordan River into the promised land, immediately follows the exhortation for Israel to keep itself separate from all other people, because they can lead the Israelites into idolatry. Moses reminds them that they "are a people holy to the LORD" (7:6), meaning that they have a relationship with the God they name LORD. Their God shares himself with his people; thus, they are holy as he is holy.

They also have a history with the God they name LORD. Moses explains, "It was because the LORD loved [them] and kept the oath that he swore to [their] ancestors, that the LORD has brought [them] out with a mighty hand, and redeemed [them] from the house of slavery, from the hand of Pharaoh king of Egypt" (7:8). In other words, "the LORD [their] God has chosen [them] out of all the peoples on earth to be his people, his treasured possession" (7:6). God did not choose them because they were the most numerous people; indeed, they were the fewest, but "the LORD set his heart on [them] and chose them" (7:7). Moses continues to emphasize the faithfulness of God "who maintains covenant loyalty with those who love him and keep his commandments" (7:9).

It is important for modern readers to notice that Moses' focus is on what God has done for the Israelites, not on what they did. Because we live in a culture of people who think that they make their own choices, this passage from Deuteronomy reminds us that the LORD our God chooses us, loves us, and maintains covenant loyalty with us. In other words, God makes the first move toward us, making us holy so that we can respond to his offer.

We were chosen by God to be baptized. If we were baptized as children, our parents may have presented us to the church for baptism, but it was God who chose us to die and rise to new life. God chose us again in Confirmation to receive the Holy Spirit. God calls us to celebrate the Eucharist of his Son, Jesus Christ, then he calls us to the altar-table to share in the sacrificial meal.

On this Solemnity of the Most Sacred Heart of Jesus, this passage reminds us that God loves us. It is not an infatuation love or a puppy love or friendship love with which the LORD loves us. God loves us with a sacrificial love, demonstrated in the death and resurrection of his Son, who renewed his covenant with the Jews and offered it to the Gentiles. God loves us sacrificially.

The LORD's covenant loyalty is enacted every time we celebrate a sacrament; God promises to be with us through suffering and death, through reconciliation for our failings, through marriage, through ordination to the diaconate, priesthood, or episcopacy. The new covenant sealed in the blood of Christ at every Eucharist and shared by all present is the best demonstration of God's sacrificial love for his people. Jesus continues to pour out his blood from his most sacred heart as a reminder of the LORD's choosing, his love, and his loyalty to us.

Meditation: In what specific ways have you experienced being chosen, loved by, and faithful to the LORD God?

Prayer: LORD, our God, once you chose a people and with a mighty hand you redeemed them from Egyptian slavery. In the fullness of time, you sent your Son to call all people to covenant loyalty. Grant that we may know your commandments and observe them, that we may share eternal life with you, your Son Jesus Christ, and the Holy Spirit, forever and ever. Amen.

Abide

1 John 4:7–16

Scripture: "God is love, and those who abide in love abide in God, and God abides in them" (1 John 4:16b).

Reflection: The first letter of John might also be called an in-depth reflection on God's love. In the second to last chapter of the work the author makes the statement, "In this is love, not that we loved God but that he loved us and sent his Son to be the atoning sacrifice for our sins" (4:10). In other words, God has demonstrated his love for people by taking the initiative to make the first move toward them, namely, sending "his only Son into the world so that [they] might live through him" (4:9). People, therefore, love one another "because love is from God" (4:7) and because "God loved [them] so much" (4:11). Even though God cannot be seen, when people love one another, they experience God living in them and his love being perfected in them. The way people love each other, that is, their behavior toward each other, demonstrates the reality of their relationship with God.

Another way to reflect upon this relationship with God that people have through Jesus Christ is to consider the concept of abiding. To abide means to wait for, to endure, to bear patiently, to remain stable. The author of the first letter of John states that people "know that [they] abide in [God] and he in [them], because he has given [them] of his Spirit" (4:13). Furthermore, "God abides in those who confess that Jesus is the Son of God, and they abide in God" (4:15). The experience of love is found in the abiding of the members of the community. Through Jesus and the Spirit, people are invisibly connected to each other and to the source of all life: God. Thus, "God is love, and those who abide in love abide in God, and God abides in them" (4:16).

Those who love as God does, that is, sacrificially, live in God, and God lives in them. Their behavior to one another demonstrates their remaining in God's love. God willingly sacrificed his Son for the love of people; people demonstrate their acceptance of God's offer of love by willingly sacrificing themselves for one another. "Everyone who loves is born of God and knows God" (4:7). Everyone who loves is born of God because he or she has accepted God's offer of love and abides in it. He or she knows God, because to love is to know God, who is love.

On this Solemnity of the Most Sacred Heart of Jesus, we need to raise our awareness on three levels. First, God loves us first; we do not make the first move. We respond to God's love by confessing that the Father sent his Son as the Savior of the world. Second, our response to God's love has a corollary response: We love one another, and our behavior demonstrates that we do, indeed, love one another sacrificially. In other words, we find ourselves putting others ahead of ourselves. Third, when we love one another, we are abiding in each other and in God. We wait for, endure, bear patiently, and remain stable in the love we share with others and God.

Meditation: What recent behavior of yours demonstrates that you abide in love?

Prayer: God our Father, you demonstrated your love by sending your Son into the world to be the atoning sacrifice for our sins. Even though we cannot see you, we believe that you abide in us when we confess that Jesus is your Son. Fill us with your Spirit of love, that we may love one another as you love us and have that love perfected in us. You are one God—Father, Son, and Holy Spirit—abiding in love forever and ever. Amen.

Yoke

Matthew 11:25–30

Scripture: "At that time Jesus said, . . . 'Come to me, all you that are weary and are carrying heavy burdens, and I will give you rest. Take my yoke upon you, and learn from me . . .'" (Matt 11:25, 28–29).

Reflection: A yoke is a wooden frame which joins two draft animals—usually oxen—at the necks for working together. A person may fashion a yoke and fit it to his or her shoulders in order to carry a balanced load in two equal portions. In the Judaism of Jesus' day, the Torah or Law was often referred to as a yoke. Its six hundred thirteen precepts, if embraced, served as a yoke for a person's life.

Verses 25–27 have been taken by Matthew from the same source that Luke used (10:21–22), referred to as Q (for "Quelle" meaning "source"). From his own unique source, Matthew has added verses 28–30. These verses hark back to the Sermon on the Mount in which Jesus declares, "Do not think that I have come to abolish the law or the prophets; I have come not to abolish but to fulfill" (5:17). Portrayed as a teacher of wisdom, the Matthean Jesus presents a righteousness that greatly exceeds that taught by the other wisdom teachers—scribes and Pharisees—of the time.

Jesus invites those who have grown weary of the old righteousness, the old Torah yoke, to accept his way, which is doing the right thing because it is the right thing to do. Thus, according to Jesus, anger, lust, and oaths are forbidden. Love of enemies and prayer for persecutors are prescribed. These characterize the gentle- and humble-hearted Jesus, who offers rest to his followers. Thus, his yoke is easy, and his burden is light.

In the context of today's Solemnity of the Most Sacred Heart of Jesus, the church acknowledges the higher righteousness to which we are called. Make no mistake about it: This is a yoke because it goes beyond the mere keeping of Torah to the intention of it. Thus, anger is forbidden because it separates people from each other—a type of murder. Divorce is forbidden because it leads to adultery and destroys marriages. And oaths are forbidden because personal integrity dictates that one, simply, speak the truth—and no swearing is needed to authenticate the truth. According to Jesus, his yoke is easy, because its basic principle is always doing the right thing because the right thing is the right thing to do!

Meditation: What have been three recent opportunities for you to do the right thing because it was the right thing to do, that is, practice righteousness?

Prayer: Father, Lord of heaven and earth, we praise you for having revealed your truth through your Son. Through your Holy Spirit, fill us with righteousness that we may take up Jesus' yoke and be followers of Christ in word and deed. He lives and reigns with you and the Holy Spirit, one God, forever and ever. Amen.

CYCLE B

Child

Hosea 11:1, 3–4, 8c–9

Scripture: The LORD says, ". . . It was I who taught Ephraim to walk, I took them up in my arms . . ." (Hos 11:3ab).

Reflection: The pieced-together verses that comprise the first reading from the prophet Hosea on this Solemnity of the Most Sacred Heart of Jesus is one of only a few restoration speeches. Hosea lived in the northern kingdom of Israel and prophesied there during the last thirty years of its existence (750 BC–721 BC) before Assyria conquered it and scattered the ten tribes of the people.

In the midst of many speeches condemning Ephraim—another name for Israel—for its faithlessness, Hosea employs the image of a child, portraying God as the parent. "When Israel was a child, I loved him, and out of Egypt I called my son" (11:1), writes the prophet. Just as a parent teaches a child to walk, so God "taught Ephraim to walk" and took up the people in his arms (11:3). God was "like those who lift infants to their cheeks" (11:4), like one who bends down to feed them.

After presenting the image of a child and himself as the parent, the LORD asks himself a series of questions: "How can I give you up, Ephraim? How can I hand you over, O Israel?" (11:8). The questions are omitted from the Lectionary. After considering his questions, God, declares, "I will not execute my fierce anger; I will not again destroy Ephraim" (11:9). The LORD has decided to restore the people, according to Hosea. However, this hope of restoration never took place.

The Lectionary omits from today's passage the verses of judgment. In 11:2, the LORD states, "The more I called [Israel], the more they went from me; they kept sacrificing to the Baals, and offering incense to idols." Likewise, God's declaration that Israel will return to a state of Egyptian slavery because Assyria will rule them along with words about the ravages of the sword and more (11:5–7) are omitted from the pericope in order to present only the child-parent metaphor.

Solemnity of the Most Sacred Heart of Jesus

On this Solemnity of the Most Sacred Heart of Jesus we are invited to enter the metaphor. God our Father brings us to birth, fosters a relationship with us, loves us, raises us with kindness, and feeds us. We may forget that we exist because the LORD wills it. In our arrogance we can come to think that we supply our own needs; we forget that we are the child and God is the parent. As the passage illustrates, God's heart is broken when his people reject him and refuse to return to him. Hosea notes God saying, "My heart recoils within me; my compassion grows warm and tender" (11:8). And so it is even now in the person of God's Son, Jesus Christ. Using the metaphor of his most sacred heart, Jesus indicates that it is broken, yet he desires that all people go to him.

Meditation: In what ways are you like a rebellious child called to return to God?

Prayer: Most High God, you so loved your chosen people that you set them free from Egyptian slavery and brought them to the land promised to Abraham and Sarah and their descendants. You further revealed your love for all people through the suffering and death of your Son. With chords of grace draw us deeper into your life and your kingdom, where you live as one God—Father, Son, and Holy Spirit—forever and ever. Amen.

Christ's Love

Ephesians 3:8–12, 14–19

Scripture: "I [, Paul,] pray that you [, Ephesians,] may have the power to comprehend, with all the saints, what is the breadth and length and height and depth, and to know the love of Christ that surpasses knowledge, so that you may be filled with all the fullness of God" (Eph 3:18–19).

Reflection: The second-generation Pauline letter known as the letter to the Ephesians and written around 80 AD presents material that takes the historical Paul's ideas and makes them relevant for a new generation of believers. Today's passage presents part of Paul's reflections on his ministry

(3:8–12) and part of his prayer (3:14–19). Because the context for both are not given in the Lectionary, confusion can be the result of today's pericope.

Earlier in the reflection on his ministry, Paul explains that his role has brought him to imprisonment "for Christ Jesus for the sake of . . . Gentiles . . ." (3:1). Paul, whom we remember was a radical Jew set on eliminating Christianity from the face of the earth, makes a very bold statement. In the past God did not reveal "the mystery of Christ" (3:4) to people, "as it has now been revealed to his holy apostles and prophets by the Spirit; that is, the Gentiles have become fellow heirs, members of the same body, and sharers in the promise of Christ Jesus through the gospel" (3:5–6). Paul has been a servant of this gospel "according to the gift of God's grace that was given [him] by the working of this power" (3:7).

Paul continues with words about grace that form the beginning of today's pericope. God's grace was given to him "to bring to the Gentiles the news of the boundless riches of Christ, and to make everyone see what is the plan of the mystery hidden for ages in God who created all things" (3:8–9). In other words, Paul's mission has been to acknowledge that God's plan to save Jews and Gentiles and reconcile them to each other and to God has existed from the beginning. God has accomplished his eternal purpose through Christ. Now, "through the church the wisdom of God in its rich variety" (11:10) makes known this mystery to everyone.

Following his reflections on ministry, Paul breaks into prayer, bending his knees "before the Father, from whom every family in heaven and on earth takes its name" (11:14–15). The prayer asks that the readers be strengthened in their "inner being with power through [the Father's] Spirit, and that Christ may dwell in [their] hearts through faith, as [they] are rooted and grounded in love" (3:16–17). Paul also asks that the readers comprehend the big picture, the mystery he has been writing about, "so that [they] may be filled with all the fullness of God" (3:19). The Lectionary omits the last two verses of the prayer which form a doxology.

This edited passage is presented on the Solemnity of the Most Sacred Heart of Jesus because the prayer begs God to ground believers in love so that they know "the love of Christ that surpasses knowledge" (3:19). The heart of Jesus, a sign of his love for all people, serves as a metaphor for these second-generation words of Paul.

Love for Paul is not cultural infatuation or teenage love. Paul understands that God demonstrated his love for all people through the death and resurrection of his own Son. Love is the willingness to sacrifice one's life for the good of others. Jesus did that, and those adapting original Paul in thought near the end of the first century exhort others to do the same. Grounded in sacrificial love, they will know the love of Christ that surpasses all knowledge, and, just as God raised Jesus from the dead, those who know Christ's love will be filled with God's fullness.

Meditation: In what specific sacrificial acts of love have you been able to experience God's fullness?

Prayer: God of love, we bow our knees before you and pray that you will strengthen our inner being with power through your Holy Spirit that your Son, our Lord Jesus Christ, may dwell in our hearts through faith. Grant that we may know the love of Christ and be filled with your fullness. He is Lord forever and ever. Amen.

Open Side

John 19:31–37

Scripture: "... [O]ne of the soldiers pierced [Jesus'] side with a spear, and at once blood and water came out" (John 19:34).

Reflection: In John's Gospel, Jesus is portrayed as a new passover lamb. He dies on the cross at the same time as the lambs were being slaughtered in the Temple in preparation for passover. Beside the image of Jesus as the new passover lamb is the image of Jesus as a new man. While the authors of John's Gospel do not develop this latter metaphor as well as Paul does in his letters, it is indicated in the sign of the soldier piercing the side of the dead Jesus with a spear and blood and water coming out.

In the second creation account in the book of Genesis, the author narrates that the LORD God, after causing a deep sleep to fall upon the man, "took one of his ribs and closed up its place with flesh" (2:21). Out of that rib from the man's side God created a woman. The authors of John's Gospel have that story in mind when they write, "... [O]ne of the soldiers pierced [Jesus'] side with a spear, and at once blood and water came out" (19:34).

Like the man from whom a rib is taken and fashioned into a woman, from the side of Christ pours out two sacraments that give birth to the church. Water, a sign of baptism, appears in almost every Johannine story. Nicodemus is told that he must be born again of water and the Spirit. The woman of Samaria goes to Jacob's well to get water only to meet Jesus, who gives her living water. In a pool, the man washes away the mud Jesus smeared on his blind eyes and is able to see. And on and on the stories go with the theme of the life-giving characteristic of water.

Blood is not as exploited as water in John's Gospel. It does appear in the Bread of Life discourse, where Jesus tells his followers to drink his blood. At the wedding in Cana, Jesus changed six jars of water into wine, which was used to represent blood. As such blood/wine becomes a sign of Eucharist. So, when blood flows out of his side after his death on the cross, eternal life is flowing for all to drink.

In the context of this Solemnity of the Most Sacred Heart of Jesus, we celebrate the love that God has shown us through Jesus' death on the cross, his pierced side, and his birthing of the church through baptism and Eucharist. We are reminded of our baptism every time we enter a church and dip our hand into the water in the baptismal font. We are reminded of Eucharist every time we say, "Amen," to the minister's "The blood of Christ," and drink from the chalice. The love of Christ continues to flow from his pierced side, filling us with new life.

Meditation: How many ways do baptism and Eucharist fill you with life? Make a list.

Prayer: Eternal Father, on the Day of Preparation for Passover your Son gave his life for the world when water and blood flowed from his open side. Fill us with a greater appreciation for his selfless love, that looking upon the One who was pierced we may be filled with eternal life. We ask this through our Lord Jesus Christ, who lives and reigns with you, Father, and the Holy Spirit, one God, forever and ever. Amen.

Solemnity of the Most Sacred Heart of Jesus

CYCLE C

Shepherd

Ezekiel 34:11–16

Scripture: "I myself will be the shepherd of my sheep, and I will make them lie down, says the Lord GOD" (Ezek 34:15).

Reflection: The prophet Ezekiel writes during the Babylonian Exile of the Jews. Today's pericope is part of a longer "word of the LORD" (34:1) that came to the prophet and that indicts the leaders—understood to be the kings of Judah—for not properly taking care of God's people. The operative metaphor that is exploited throughout the passage is that of shepherd and sheep.

Because the kings pastured and fed themselves instead of pasturing and feeding the people, God declares that he will now take responsibility to "search for [his] sheep, and . . . seek them out" (34:11). They have been scattered by the Babylonians, but God "will bring them from the countries, and will bring them into their own land" (34:13). Emphatically, God declares, "I myself will be the shepherd of my sheep, and I will make them lie down, says the Lord GOD" (34:15).

In the midst of the destruction of Jerusalem and its temple and the deportation of the Jews to Babylon, Ezekiel offers hope that one day the people will return to the land of Israel. God will replace the Davidic line of shepherds with himself, because the monarchy was effectively destroyed by Nebuchadnezzar, King of Babylon. Ezekiel's words make the lyrics of Psalm 23:1 a hope: "The LORD is my shepherd, I shall not want."

Because most people today have no experience of sheep, the drama of Ezekiel's prophecy can be easily glossed over. Repeatedly throughout biblical literature people are referred to as sheep without a shepherd. Anyone who knows anything about sheep concludes that this is an insult. Basically, the metaphor identifies people as stupid, helpless, and ignorant. The kings of Israel and Judah were commissioned to be primarily concerned about God's chosen people. Over the course of time, however, politics, greed, and the desire for an heir pushed what was supposed to be their primary concern to the back of the line. Finally, this led to their conquest by the

Assyrians, who defeated the Kingdom of Israel, and then the Babylonians, who defeated the Kingdom of Judah.

Living in exile with the Jews, Ezekiel declares that God is taking over the role of shepherd. He will gather the exiles and bring them back to Jerusalem; he will feed them and make them prosper; he will find the lost and heal the injured. And most importantly, the Lord GOD states, "I will feed them with justice" (34:16). In other words, God declares that he will give to his people what is due to them. In time, God raised up Cyrus of Persia, who defeated the Babylonians and permitted the Jews to return to Jerusalem.

God shepherds us today through the pope and bishop and pastor he sends us. The pope shepherds the universal church, reading the signs of the times and guiding her morally, liturgically, and politically. The local bishop is a shepherd, teaching, sanctifying, and governing the flock of a diocese entrusted to his care. The bishop appoints pastors, who are responsible for guiding the parish flock. Various leadership skills and styles exist, but the goal is always to lead, guide, or push the sheep toward God. This is no easy task in a culture that fosters rugged individualism among the members of the church, which fosters rugged community (flock). On this Solemnity of the Most Sacred Heart of Jesus we do well to reflect on our ability or our stubbornness to be shepherded by those whom God sends to us.

Meditation: In what ways are you shepherded?

Prayer: Lord GOD, eternal shepherd, we do not want because you lead us to verdant pastures and refresh our souls. You spread your table before us with the body and blood of your Son, and you invite us to dwell in your house for ever. Through the Holy Spirit, keep us faithful to Jesus Christ, who lives and reigns with you and the Holy Spirit, one God, forever and ever. Amen.

Daring Death

Romans 5:5b–11

Scripture: "Indeed, rarely will anyone die for a righteous person—though perhaps for a good person someone might actually dare to die" (Rom 5:7).

Solemnity of the Most Sacred Heart of Jesus

Reflection: Today's passage from Paul's letter to the Romans is part of a longer summary of the results of being justified by faith, which act of God is a demonstration of his love. Furthermore, "God's love has been poured into [believers'] hearts through the Holy Spirit that has been given to [them]" (5:5).

Here's how justification by faith works: God makes the first move toward people. Paul states, ". . . [W]hile we were still weak, at the right time Christ died for the ungodly" (5:6). The "ungodly"—otherwise known as sinners—are those who oppose God. However, ". . . God proves his love for us in that while we still were sinners Christ died for us" (5:8). How's that for a demonstration of God's love for those who oppose him?! In fact, as Paul reflects, "Indeed, rarely will anyone die for a righteous person—though perhaps for a good person someone might actually dare to die" (5:7). Christ's death demonstrates how much God loves people, even sinners.

The blood of Christ was God's move to justify all sinners, that is, all people, so that they could "be saved through [Christ] from the wrath of God" (5:9). Now, Paul presents one of his typical "how much more" arguments, stating, "For if while we were enemies, we were reconciled to God through the death of his Son, much more surely, having been reconciled, will we be saved by his life" (5:10). In other words, if this is what God did for us when we were alienated from him, namely, reconcile us to himself, we can be hopefully confident that the resurrection life that God gave to Christ is a further demonstration of our salvation.

We do not boast of what we have accomplished, because we have done nothing! God decided to reconcile us and made reconciliation possible through the death of his Son. Then, God made new life possible by raising Christ from the dead. All this has been done for us by God and offered to us. So, all we can do is "boast in God through our Lord Jesus Christ, through whom we have now received reconciliation" (5:11). Standing in this grace, this gift, gives us hope of sharing the glory of God.

On this Solemnity of the Most Sacred Heart of Jesus we should discover ourselves standing in grace and being overwhelmed by God's love manifest in Christ Jesus' death for us sinners. God's love caused him to make the first move to justify his people by faith. Instead of boasting of what we have done, we need to boast of what God has done through our Lord Jesus Christ.

Meditation: What has God done for you that you need to boast about him through Jesus Christ?

Prayer: Almighty Father, while we still were sinners, your Son died for us. The cross is the sign of your love for us. The new life of Christ's resurrection is our hope of sharing in your glory. Overwhelm our awareness of this graced gift that we may never cease to praise you, Father, through your Son, Jesus Christ, in the unity of the Holy Spirit, forever and ever. Amen.

Lost Sheep

Luke 15:3–7

Scripture: [Jesus asked the Pharisees and scribes:] "Which one of you, having a hundred sheep and losing one of them, does not leave the ninety-nine in the wilderness and go after the one that is lost until he finds it?" (Luke 15:4)

Reflection: The narrative known as the parable of the lost sheep comes from Q (from "Quelle," meaning "source"), used by both Matthew and Luke when they composed their gospels. Each gives it a different setting; Luke groups it with two other parables about lost things, namely, a lost coin and a lost son. As far as the author of Luke's Gospel is concerned, the structure of the lost sheep, the lost coin, and the lost son parables contains the same theme: what is lost is found.

As is any parable, the lost sheep illustrates the outrageous. When Jesus asks the Pharisees and scribes, "Which one of you, having a hundred sheep and losing one of them, does not leave the ninety-nine in the wilderness and go after the one that is lost until he finds it?" (15:4), they immediately think, "No one." Correct. No shepherd would leave ninety-nine sheep in the desert and go look for one; when he returned with the one, he'd have only one! If he did not find the one, he would find none left, because all the sheep would have scattered. This parable could have stopped after its opening question.

But it becomes even more outrageous. The man finds the sheep, puts it on his shoulders, rejoicing, and gathers his friends and neighbors and has a joyful party. No mention is made of the ninety-nine sheep left in the desert!

The application is now supplied. The one lost sheep, who cannot know it was lost, has been found. People are like sheep; they don't know they are lost until someone finds them. Have you ever had a friend who was lost? You found him and gave him a sense of direction with some good advice. Maybe it was a child who was lost; you took her on a walk and talked and talked until you found her. In marriage, one party often gets lost—through drugs, alcohol, technology—and the other partner finds him or her, raising awareness and getting help.

The ninety-nine righteous do not need to be found because they are not lost. Jesus found sinners and ate with them—outrageous acts if there ever were any!—in order to find them. He was good at finding them. In marking the Solemnity of the Most Sacred Heart of Jesus, we remember all the lost who have been found by Christ working through his body, the church, us. When a lost one is found, we want to rejoice.

Meditation: Who has found you? Why were you lost?

Prayer: Eternal Shepherd, you never leave your flock unguarded. Through the ministry of your Son, you have sought out the lost. Continue this ministry through us, your church. Guide us with the Holy Spirit that we may gather into one all those who have been scattered. We ask this through our Lord Jesus Christ, your Son, who lives and reigns with you and the Holy Spirit, one God, forever and ever. Amen.

✠ Saturday Following the Second Sunday after Pentecost
Memorial of the Immaculate Heart
of the Blessed Virgin Mary

Heart

Luke 2:41–51

Scripture: "[The child Jesus] went down [from Jerusalem] with [his parents] and came to Nazareth, and was obedient to them. His mother treasured all these things in her heart..." (Luke 2:51).

Reflection: Luke's Gospel presents two parallel stories concerning the childhood of Jesus. The first is the presentation in the Temple (2:22–40). The second, today's proper gospel passage, is the trip to Jerusalem for Passover when Jesus is twelve years old. After keeping Passover and spending one day traveling home to Nazareth, Jesus' parents discover that he is not with the group of travelers. Backtracking, they find him after three days "in the Temple, sitting among the teachers, listening to them and asking them questions" (2:46).

Joseph has not been named or identified since the beginning of this chapter (2:4, 2:16, and before these verses only at 1:27) because the author's focus has been, and continues to be, on Jesus' mother, Mary. His mother questions him about his behavior, and he responds: "Why were you searching for me? Did you not know that I must be in my Father's house?" (2:49) His parents do not understand his answer. However, he joins them in returning to Nazareth. Meanwhile, "His mother treasured all these things in her heart" (2:51), much like she had after the shepherds had visited the new-born child (2:19).

This pericope is chosen for this memorial because it mentions the heart of Jesus' mother. Today's memorial, coming as it does on the day after

Memorial of the Immaculate Heart of the Blessed Virgin Mary

the Solemnity of the Most Sacred Heart of Jesus, remembers the immaculate—that is, the pure—heart of the Blessed Virgin Mary. Mary stands open to the will of God and the marvels of God. She ponders the events surrounding the birth of her Son, and she reflects upon the events surrounding his being lost and found in the Temple in Jerusalem, not to mention the words he speaks to her.

Mary is a model for Christian reflection. She carefully examines the events of her life in the hope of seeing God's fingerprints all over them. Mary understands that Divine revelation continues throughout history. We, too, need to take time, to sit quietly—turning off all cell phones, radios, TVs, computers—and reflect on our day. Where did we discover God's activity in our lives? In our morning routine? At our place of work? During our lunch-time discussion? While commuting home in the evening? With family members while eating dinner? Without reflecting on the events of our lives, we miss the revelation of the presence of God. By reflecting on the events of our lives, we begin to recognize all the leading and guiding God does in and through us, and, like Mary, we store these things in our hearts.

Meditation: What most recent event in your life was a manifestation of God's presence?

Prayer: God of Jesus, the mother of your Son, Mary, pondered the events of her life in order to recognize your work in saving the world. Through your Holy Spirit, enable us to name the revelations of your love in our lives and store them in our hearts. We ask this through our Lord Jesus Christ, who lives and reigns with you and the Holy Spirit, one God, forever and ever. Amen.

✤ June 11
Memorial of St. Barnabas, Apostle

Obedient

Acts 11:21b–26; 13:1–3

Scripture: ". . . [T]he church in Jerusalem . . . sent Barnabas to Antioch. When he came and saw the grace of God, he rejoiced, and he exhorted them all to remain faithful to the Lord with steadfast devotion; for he was a good man, full of the Holy Spirit of faith" (Acts 11:22–24a).

Reflection: In the Acts of the Apostles, both Barnabas and Paul are named apostles in addition to the eleven and Matthias. While the day honoring Barnabas as an apostle is not a feast, like those of the rest of the apostles, this memorial provides the opportunity to reflect upon the activity of Barnabas through this pieced-together pericope.

The author of the Acts of the Apostles introduces Barnabas in chapter 4, identifying him as "a Levite, a native of Cyprus," whose name was Joseph, "to whom the apostles gave the name Barnabas (which means 'son of encouragement')" (4:36). Barnabas sold a field and gave the money to the apostles. He is also responsible for introducing Saul (Paul) to the apostles in Jerusalem (9:27). After this Barnabas becomes Paul's companion and is always mentioned in a sentence by the author as being with Paul (11:29–30, 12:25; 13:1, 2, 7, 42, 43, 46, 50; 14:1, 12, 14, 20; 15:2, 12, 22, 25, 35, 36, 37) until they have a disagreement and part company; "Barnabas . . . sailed away to Cyprus" (15:39), from where he came.

Today's passage narrates the spreading of the gospel to the Hellenists in Antioch. When this news reached Jerusalem, the apostles sent Barnabas to Antioch, which will become the base for Paul's missionary work. Barnabas exhorts the new believers "to remain faithful to the Lord with steadfast devotion" (11:23). The author tells us that Barnabas "was a good man, full of the Holy Spirit and of faith" (11:24). Next, Barnabas goes to Tarsus, finds Paul, and brings him to Antioch, from where the two will set out together on many evangelizing mission trips.

After skipping all of chapter 12, today's passage continues with a description of the "church at Antioch" in which there are "prophets and teachers" (13:1) among whom are Barnabas and Saul (Paul). While all are "worshiping the Lord and fasting, the Holy Spirit" says, "Set apart for me Barnabas and Saul for the work to which I have called them" (13:2). Then, after the others had fasted and prayed, "they laid their hands on them and sent them off" (13:3). Thus, the first missionary journey of Barnabas and Paul, like that of the other apostles at Pentecost, is launched by the Holy Spirit.

Luke, the author of the Acts of the Apostles, portrays Barnabas as obedient to the Holy Spirit's call. With Paul he sets out on their first missionary journey to be obedient to the proclamation of the gospel. And this is where Barnabas becomes a model for us today. The word of God needs proclaimers; in order for people to hear God's word, men and women must hear it themselves, believe it, and live it. St. Francis of Assisi once told his friars, "Spread the gospel wherever you go; use words when necessary." The *Catechism of the Catholic Church* emphasizes this point, too, stating: "Lay people . . . fulfill their prophetic mission by evangelization, 'that is, the proclamation of Christ by word and the testimony of life.' For lay people, 'this evangelization . . . acquires a specific property and peculiar efficacy because it is accomplished in the ordinary circumstances of the world'" (905).

Reflection: In what specific ways are you a proclaimer of the gospel?

Prayer: Ever-living God, through the Holy Spirit your summoned Barnabas to be an apostle of your Son, and he responded in obedience by proclaiming your word. Make us attentive to the Scriptures, that we may proclaim that Jesus Christ is Lord in word and deed to the ends of the world. We ask this through the same Christ, our Lord. Amen.

Proclaim

Matthew 10:7–13

Scripture: Jesus said to his twelve disciples, "As you go, proclaim the good news, 'The kingdom of heaven has come near'" (Matt 10:7).

Reflection: The seven verses comprising the gospel passage for the Memorial of St. Barnabas are taken from the second major discourse that Jesus delivers in Matthew's Gospel. The Matthean Jesus delivers five major discourses or sermons which are meant to portray him as a new Moses, who, according to tradition, wrote the first five books of the Bible, collectively known as the Torah.

After naming the twelve apostles, the Matthean Jesus instructs them about missionary activity. Matthew adds to the missionary material he found in Mark's Gospel. Specifically, he adds the proclamation of the nearness of the kingdom of heaven. This was the announcement of John the Baptist earlier in the gospel, and it is the announcement of Jesus after his baptism. Matthew wants his reader to understand that there is continuity between John, Jesus, and the apostles.

More continuity exists in the four commands to cure, to raise, to cleanse, and to cast out. In chapters 8 and 9, this is exactly what Jesus has done. The apostles continue his work with their missionary activity.

Another unique verse to Matthew's missionary command is this: "You received without payment; give without payment" (10:8). God, who is the giver of all gifts, desires that those who follow his Son give away his gifts as freely as he gives them to the apostles. No one can lay claim to God's gifts; they are on loan to missionaries, who rely upon God for money, clothes, food, lodging, and peace.

Reliance upon God seems to be a thing of the past. Modern people seem to rely upon themselves for everything they need. This means that they have to work for everything. Once they have met their needs, then they can prepare for the mission. However, that seems to be where the mission work gets lost. Modern people never have enough—time, money, clothes, food, space, etc.—to ever get started.

The Memorial of St. Barnabas, companion of St. Paul in the Acts of the Apostles, calls all to the mission entrusted to them on the day of baptism. All are sent with the announcement of the kingdom of heaven. Baptism makes us the next in the continuous line from John the Baptist to Jesus to the apostles to us. The kingdom is here now; we demonstrate its presence both by the words we speak and the way we live our lives. We demonstrate it by our reliance upon God for everything. We demonstrate it by putting the mission of its proclamation at the top of our list.

Meditation: In what specific ways do you announce that God's kingdom is here?

Prayer: Almighty God, the Holy Spirit set aside Barnabas to accompany Paul on his journeys to announce the presence of your kingdom. Remove all that hinders us from bringing the good news of your Son, Jesus Christ, to the area in which we live. Without cost we have received; grant that without cost we give. Hear this prayer through the same Jesus Christ, who is Lord forever and ever. Amen.

✤ July 3
Feast of St. Thomas, Apostle

Temple

Ephesians 2:19-22

Scripture: "In [Christ Jesus] the whole structure is joined together and grows into a holy temple in the Lord . . ." (Eph 2:21).

Reflection: In chapter two of the letter to the Ephesians, the post-Pauline writer reminds the Gentiles that at one time they were without Christ, but through the blood of Christ they have been brought into union with all people who believe that Jesus died and God raised him from the dead. It is by grace—a pure gift of God—that Gentiles have been saved through faith. No one can be saved by works; that is, no one can earn salvation. All people can do is accept the gift that God offers to them.

Through Christ, Gentiles have access to the Father in one Spirit. This makes them strangers and aliens no longer. Now they are citizen-saints, believers, members of God's household. God is the father of this family, and all are brothers and sisters in it.

The post-Pauline author of the letter changes his metaphor from household/family to temple. The foundation stones of the temple consist of apostles and prophets. The cornerstone is Christ Jesus. Every member is like a stone of the structure that is cemented together on top of the foundation stones. The spiritual cement is the Holy Spirit. In this temple, God dwells.

In a culture of the individual, the post-Pauline author's one temple imagery may be lost. The temple does not consist of many temples, but only one joined together by the Holy Spirit from both Jews and Gentiles and built on the foundation of apostles and prophets with Christ Jesus as the

Feast of St. Thomas, Apostle

cornerstone. In this Trinitarian building lives God, who has chosen people to be united as his dwelling place.

The Feast of St. Thomas, an apostle, provides the opportunity to examine our place in God's temple. All of us together form the structure on the foundation of Thomas and the other apostles. No one of us is any more or less important than anyone else. The good of the whole temple comes first; the individual does not place his or her good above that of the whole building.

While everything around us shouts, "It's about me," today's passage from Ephesians declares, "It's about us." Specifically, "It's about God." God made us to know, to love, and to serve him in this world and to be happy with him in the next. We do this together as one temple in which the Holy One dwells.

Meditation: What is your place in God's temple? How does it foster the common good?

Prayer: Heavenly Father, your Son, Jesus Christ, called Thomas to follow him as an apostle. With Thomas and his companions you have laid a foundation upon which you have built a temple out of all believers. Strengthen the mortar of your house with the Holy Spirit. May we be found praising you, Father, Son, and Holy Spirit, forever and ever. Amen.

Twin

John 20:24–29

Scripture: ". . . Thomas (who was called the Twin), one of the twelve, was not with [the disciples] when Jesus came" [on the evening of that day, the first day of the week] (John 20:24).

Reflection: John's Gospel is filled with signs; a sign is a thing that points toward another thing. Today's gospel pericope is the third scene of the Johannine post-resurrection narrative. The first scene is Jesus' appearance to Mary Magdalene; the second scene is Jesus' appearance to the disciples without Thomas behind locked doors; and the third scene is Jesus' appearance to the disciples with Thomas. After the third scene, there is short epilogue and the first ending of the gospel. Later, another author added chapter 21 and the second ending to the work.

Throughout John's Gospel, Thomas, like several other characters, makes three appearances. He invites his fellow disciples to go and die with Jesus as Jesus prepares to go raise Lazarus from the dead (11:16). After Jesus has begun his farewell discourse, explaining that he is going to prepare a place for his disciples in his Father's house, Thomas declares, "Lord, we don't know where you are going! How can we know the way?" (14:5) Thomas' third appearance in the gospel is in the third scene of the post-resurrection series of events.

Thomas is a sign, representing those who need signs to believe. After all, that has been the progression of the gospel to this point. Jesus changes water into wine, and people believe in him. He tells a woman of Samaria that he can give her living water, and she believes in him and brings others to faith in him. He heals a blind man, and people believe in him. The natural sequence is that Thomas must see the risen Christ in order to believe in him.

However, once this sequence is established—see a sign and believe—how do the authors stop it? In other words, once Jesus stops giving signs, how will people believe? The occasion of Thomas' profession of faith ("My Lord and my God!" [20:28]) is simultaneously the occasion for the Johannine Jesus to stop the sequence of sign-faith. Jesus says to Thomas: "Have you believed because you have seen me? Blessed are those who have not seen and yet have come to believe!" (20:29)

A beatitude is uttered: "Blessed are those who have not seen yet have come to believe!" (20:29) Those who have not seen signs—except for those in the gospel—are happy because they profess faith in the resurrection of Christ without seeing him, without a sign. And that brings us to the present celebration of the Feast of St. Thomas, Apostle.

Thomas is often referred to as the "Twin," but we are never told who his twin was. We can be Thomas' twin in either one of two ways. We can be Thomas' twin in needing to see a sign in order to believe that God raised Jesus from the dead. Or we can be Thomas' blessed twin by believing without seeing. The author of John's Gospel prefers the latter twinning.

Meditation: In what way are you Thomas' twin?

Feast of St. Thomas, Apostle

Prayer: After he spent three days in the tomb, you raised your Son from death to life, Almighty Father, and granted that he be seen by Mary Magdalene and his disciples. As we celebrate the Feast of St. Thomas, give us a faith that is so strong that it does not need signs to profess that Jesus Christ is Lord and God, forever and ever. Amen.

✠ July 22
Memorial of St. Mary Magdalene

Female Apostle

John 20:1-2, 11-18

Scripture: "[Mary Magdalene] turned around and saw Jesus standing there [by the tomb], but she did not know that it was Jesus. Jesus said to her, 'Woman, why are you weeping? Whom are you looking for?' Supposing him to be the gardener, she said to him, 'Sir, if you have carried him away, tell me where you have laid him, and I will take him away.' Jesus said to her, 'Mary!' She turned and said to him in Hebrew, 'Rabbouni!' (which means Teacher)" (John 20:14–16).

Reflection: Unique to John's Gospel is the narrative of the risen Jesus' encounter with Mary Magdalene, who is mentioned as one of the three Marys standing at the cross (19:25) and as going alone to the tomb on the first day of the week (20:1) and discovering that the stone has been taken away from its entrance to Jesus' tomb. Known in Christian history as the apostle (one sent) to the apostles, she runs to tell Simon Peter what she has discovered, then she returns to the tomb to stand weeping outside it.

Mary Magdalene glances into the tomb and sees "two angels in white, sitting where the body of Jesus had been lying, one at the head and the other at the feet" (20:12). They ask her about her tears, and she explains that she is looking for the body of Jesus. Turning around, she sees Jesus standing there, but she does not recognize him in his risen body. Jesus asks her the same question as the angels asked, "Woman, why are you weeping? Whom are you looking for?" (20:15) The author of the narrative informs the reader that she thinks he must be the gardener, who has removed the body from

Memorial of St. Mary Magdalene

the tomb for some unidentified reason. She asks him to indicate where he put the body, and she will take it away.

However, Jesus pronounces her name. And calling her by name enables her to recognize him. Serving her role as apostle to the apostle, Jesus sends her to his brothers to tell them that he is raised and that he is ascending to God. As the narrator states, "Mary Magdalene went and announced to the disciples, 'I've seen the Lord'; and she told them that he had said these things to her" (20:18). Thus, she fulfills her role as apostle to the apostles.

The narrative concerning Mary Magdalene's encounter with the risen Christ serves as a model for us. There is a process in the account. First, Mary Magdalene mourns the death of her Lord; she is emotionally upset when she discovers the open tomb without a corpse. Second, her mourning clouds her recognition of the very one she seeks. In other words, she is so focused on finding a dead body that she cannot see the risen One standing before her. Third, recognition comes only when Christ calls her by name. His questions to her did not arouse recognition, but the pronouncement of her name did. Fourth, she responds with faith, calling Jesus "Teacher" (Rabbi or Rabbouni in Hebrew), a name used extensively for Jesus by the authors of John's Gospel. Fifth, she is sent as an apostle; she has good news to bring to the disciples.

We may be mourning or bent out of shape or disillusioned by some event in our lives. Such bad days cloud our recognition of the Divine in our lives. But either through another or by direct intervention, we hear our name called by the Father, the Son, or the Holy Spirit, and we respond with faith, which changes—or should change—our perception of reality. Once we see God present—even in the stress of the day—we are re-commissioned as apostles and given the good news to bring to others. With a little reflection, it is easy to see how this process works in our lives.

Meditation: After choosing a recent event in your life, identify (1) the mourning, (2) the clouding, (3) the recognition of the Divine Presence, (4) the faith, and (5) the sending that occurred.

Prayer: God and Father, your apostle Mary Magdalene came to recognize your Son in his risen body after he called her name. Open our ears to hear his voice. Give us your Spirit to help us recognize his presence. Send us to others with the good news that Jesus Christ lives and reigns with you and the Holy Spirit, one God, forever and ever. Amen.

✤ July 25
Feast of St. James, Apostle

Treasure

2 Corinthians 4:7–15

Scripture: "... [W]e have this treasure in clay jars, so that it may be made clear that this extraordinary power belongs to God and does not come from us" (2 Cor 4:7).

Reflection: Everyone who believes that Jesus died and God raised him from the dead is like a clay jar in whom dwells the gospel, the good news of Christ's resurrection. According to Paul in his second letter to the Corinthians, this is an "extraordinary power" that "belongs to God and does not come from" people (2 Cor 4:7). God's glory has been revealed in the person of Jesus Christ; those who believe this are clay jars that hold this treasure. They are clay jars because one day they will die and be raised to fullness of life with him.

In the meantime, there are the afflictions of daily life; the car won't start, the air conditioner quit at home, a water pipe burst and flooded the bathroom. The living of our Christianity can bring about sneers from others who cannot understand our fasts and abstentions from meat, our natural law ethics, and our positions on political issues. Friendships may end, gasoline prices may continue to increase, and playground bullies may continue to harass our children, but all this—and more—is the way we carry "in the body the death of Jesus, so that the life of Jesus may also be made visible in our bodies" (4:10).

For Paul, dying is a lifetime process! However, none of it can put an end to the treasure we carry in our earthen jars. The more we imitate Jesus in dying, the more life of Jesus becomes visible in our mortal flesh. In a

Feast of St. James, Apostle

culture where everyone thinks he or she will live forever, Paul's words serve as an antidote. Paul reminds us that our jars are clay—they will die—but they contain a treasure of life and light that will live forever if we remain faithful to the gospel.

Celebrating the Feast of St. James, an apostle, is a statement of that fact. James believed the preaching of Jesus and followed him. With Peter and John, his brother, he witnesses the curing of Peter's mother-in-law, the raising of Jairus' daughter, and the transfiguration. At the time of Jesus' agony in the garden, James is asked to keep watch. He is martyred around 44 AD. The gospel was his treasure in his clay jar.

St. James is venerated in Spain. "Santiago de Compostela" means "St. James of the Field of Stars;" it refers to an ancient legend that a shepherd was guided to St. James' bones by starlight. Thousands of pilgrims walk the Camino, the Way, from the French Pyrenees to Spanish Compostela over several months every year to honor him.

Meditation: In what specific ways does your clay jar disclose the treasure you contain?

Prayer: Almighty Father, your Son called James the fisherman to follow him; he abandoned his father and nets and became a disciple of Jesus. Fill our clay jars with the same faith as St. James. May this treasure be our hope now and into eternity. We ask this through our Lord Jesus Christ, your Son, who lives and reigns with you and the Holy Spirit, one God forever and ever. Amen.

Mother's Request

Matthew 20:20–28

Scripture: "... [T]he mother of the sons of Zebedee came up to [Jesus] with her sons, and kneeling before him, she asked a favor of him. And he said to her, 'What do you want?' She said to him, 'Declare that these two sons of mine will sit, one at your right hand and one at your left, in your Kingdom'" (Matt 20:20–21).

Reflection: The sons of Zebedee are James and John. Matthew's source for this story is Mark's Gospel, in which James and John themselves ask for places on Jesus' right and left. In Mark's Gospel, Jesus has just given the third indication that he is going to Jerusalem to suffer and die powerlessly when James and John request the two positions of power. Matthew keeps the setting, but portrays their mother requesting the spots on either side of Jesus. Throughout Matthew's Gospel, key disciples, like James and John, are characterized in a better light than they are in Mark's Gospel.

Nevertheless, Jesus uses the occasion to teach his lesson again, namely, that his kingdom is not about power; it is about suffering and death, drinking from the cup. Being rejected characterizes Jesus' disciples—not sitting on his right and left. The Matthean Jesus makes it clear that the brothers will suffer, be rejected, and die for him. However, he does not appoint places in the Father's kingdom; God does that.

Once the other ten learn of James' and John's mother's request, they become angry with the two of them. Jesus teaches very clearly that those who are great must be servants; those who want to be first must be slaves of all. They are to imitate Jesus, who came not to be served but to serve, and to give his life as a ransom for many.

If apostles had trouble learning this lesson, how much more difficult is it for modern people to learn it. All suffering is to be eradicated as quickly as possible with an over-the-counter drug. Instead of standing for values and defending them to others which will result in rejection, we often let others voice whatever they think without us saying a word, even though we know they are wrong. And while there are those heroes who have died for others, they may do it because it is their job.

Jesus calls his disciples to greatness through suffering, rejection, and death. It is type of greatness that he displays on the cross. It is to this type of greatness that we who celebrate the feast of James are called.

Meditation: How have suffering, rejection, and death been a part of your discipleship?

Prayer: God of James, through the word and example of your Son, Jesus Christ, you called Zebedee's son to greatness through suffering, rejection, and death. Keep us faithful to the teaching of your Son through our service to others. We ask this through Christ our Lord. Amen.

✤July 29
Memorial of St. Martha

Profession of Faith

(1) John 11:19–27

Scripture: Martha said to Jesus, "... Lord, I believe that you are the Messiah, the Son of God, the one coming into the world!" (John 11:27)

Reflection: The first option of a proper gospel to mark the memorial of St. Martha is a portion of a much longer account of Jesus raising Lazarus, the response of the Pharisees, and their resolve to kill Jesus (11:1–54). A portion of this narrative is chosen for this memorial because it mentions Martha, a sister of Lazarus, by name, and because it contains Martha's supposed profession of faith.

We say "supposed" profession of faith in Jesus as the Messiah (Anointed), the Son of God, because later in the account after Jesus tells some of the Jews to remove the stone from the entrance to the tomb, "Martha, the sister of the dead man, said to [Jesus], 'Lord, already there is a stench because he has been dead four days!'" (11:39) Jesus reminds her, "Did I not tell you that if you believed, you would see the glory of God?" (11:40) On behalf of Martha, the reader has to answer "Yes" to Jesus' question.

Because today's pericope is out of context, it is easy to see that without the rest of the narrative, Martha's profession of faith that her dead brother, Lazarus, will rise "in the resurrection on the last day" (11:24), and her belief that Jesus is "the resurrection and the life" (11:25) take on a meaning they don't have in the story. As do many other characters in John's Gospel, Martha sees the sign of the raising of Lazarus and comes to believe in Jesus. Before she sees the sign, her profession of faith, while accurate, consists only of words. She is like the royal official to whom Jesus said, "Unless you see signs and wonders you will not believe" (4:48).

This is why we celebrate the biblical feast of St. Martha. If we are honest with ourselves, we know that it is easy to declare that Jesus is the resurrection and the life. It is easy to say that we believe in him, so that even if we die, we will live, and that all who live and believe in him will never die. In other words, the Nicene Creed—otherwise known as the Profession of Faith—is easy to recite Sunday after Sunday. It's when a crisis comes our direction that our faith is tested. Usually that crisis is death—a spouse, a child, a friend. In the death-denying culture of the United States of America, any death sparks immediate crisis.

Funeral arrangements need to be made; just organizing the funeral often causes sparks among family members who do not agree on what should be done. Family and friends need to be notified; delegating responsibility for this can cause more friction among the mourners. Working with the minister to prepare the funeral liturgy adds to the anxiety as options are eliminated: Scripture texts are chosen, details of the deceased's life are summarized in an obituary, and family memories are condensed. What happened to "I believe in one Lord Jesus Christ, [who] . . . suffered death and was buried, and rose again on the third day . . ."? What happened to ". . . I look forward to the resurrection of the dead and the life of the world to come"?

As Martha demonstrates, making a profession of faith is easy; living a profession of faith is a whole other story. So, on this memorial of Martha, sister of Lazarus, we may want to reflect upon the space that exists between our profession of faith and our living of faith.

Meditation: How does your faith in the resurrection enable you to process the death of family members and friends?

Prayer: Lord Jesus Christ, you are the Messiah, the Son of God, who was raised from the dead by your Father. Strengthen our profession of faith in your resurrection that we, who, like Martha, believe in you, even if we die, will live with you in the kingdom with your Father and the Holy Spirit, one God, forever and ever. Amen.

Memorial of St. Martha

One Necessary Thing

(2) Luke 10:38–42

Scripture: ". . . [T]he Lord [Jesus] answered [Martha], 'Martha, Martha, you are worried and distracted by many things; there is need of only one thing. Mary has chosen the better part, which will not be taken away from her'" (Luke 10:41–42).

Reflection: The account of Jesus entering the home of Martha and Mary is part of a much longer narrative that illustrates the Lukan theme of hearing and doing. Before this story Jesus tells the parable of the good Samaritan that illustrates doing the word—in response to a lawyer's question and answer about gaining eternal life. The Samaritan, hated by the Jews, does the word, that is, he loves his enemy, the Jew, in the ditch.

The Martha and Mary narrative illustrates the importance of hearing the word. ". . . Mary, who sat at the Lord's feet and listened to what he was saying" (10:39), obviously hears Jesus' word. He tells Martha that "there is need of only one thing" (10:41). Then he adds, "Mary has chosen the better part, which will not be taken away from her" (10:42). Thus, Mary is praised for hearing the word, but Martha is not praised for doing the word, namely, the details of hospitality, which were of the utmost importance in the ancient world.

What the author of Luke's Gospel attempts to communicate to his upper class, Gentile readers around 90 AD is that there is a time to do the word and there is a time to hear the word. While it may not be easy to determine which is which, seeing a half-dead man in a ditch is a good sign that doing the word is required. Welcoming Jesus to one's home is probably a good sign that hearing the word is required. If we bring the Scripture text into the modern world, we can say that helping the homeless, serving in the local soup kitchen, volunteering for local disaster relief are ways to do the word. Prayerfully reading the Sunday Scripture texts in preparation for Sunday Mass, spending some time in daily prayer, and reading a book about spiritual matters are ways to hear the word.

Doing does not trump hearing; hearing does not trump doing. Both are required. Hearing enables the doing; doing enables the hearing. We need both. In other words, the way to be a good Martha is to be a good Mary, and the way to be a good Mary is to be a good Martha. Martha is a good patron saint for doers of the word, while Mary is good patron saint for hearers of the word.

Meditation: How are you a doer of the word? How are you a hearer of the word?

Prayer: Loving God, through the ministry of Jesus, you have taught us to hear your word and to act on it. Give us a listening heart that we might hear you speak to us through the Scriptures. Give us strength to put into practice what we hear. We ask this through our Lord Jesus Christ, your Son, who lives and reigns with you and the Holy Spirit, one God, forever and ever. Amen.

✠ August 10
Feast of St. Lawrence, Deacon and Martyr

Steward

2 Corinthians 9:6–10

Scripture: ". . . [O]ne who sows sparingly will also reap sparingly, and the one who sows bountifully will also reap bountifully" (2 Cor 9:6).

Reflection: In today's passage from the second letter to the Corinthians, Paul is urging believers in Corinth to give generously to the collection for Jerusalem Christians. Based on an understanding that God owns everything and that people are stewards of the gifts the Holy One entrusts to them, Paul employs an agricultural metaphor. The person who sows only a few seeds will reap only a small harvest, whereas the one who sows lavishly will reap an abundant harvest. St. Francis of Assisi summarized this concept in his famous prayer, stating, "It is in giving that we receive." Another way to put it is this: What goes around comes around.

Whatever the Corinthians contribute to the collection must be deliberate; no donation can be forced. Just as all stand with open hands before God to receive, so all stand before God with open hands to give. In fact, God is the model for Paul. He states, ". . . God is able to provide you with every blessing in abundance, so that by always having enough of everything, you may share abundantly in every good work" (9:8). In other words, people give away what God has given to them in order to keep the cycle of donating going.

At the end of today's passage Paul returns to the agricultural metaphor. God supplies the seed to the sower and bread for the eater. Through people, God multiplies his bountiful graciousness insofar as they keep sharing with others what God has given to them.

This passage is read on the Feast of St. Lawrence, one of seven deacons in third-century AD Rome who was responsible for managing the church's material goods and giving to the poor. According to tradition, knowing that he was to face martyrdom, Lawrence sold all the church's material wealth and gave the money to widows, the poor, and the sick of Rome. When his murderers asked for the church's treasure, he produced those to whom he had given it, calling them the treasure of the church. For this he was martyred.

Lawrence was a worthy steward of God's gifts. Not only did he manage his master's property well, but he received blessing in abundance. He sowed bountifully and reaped a martyr's death and eternal life. Unlike many other saints who have a memorial day, St. Lawrence's celebration is ranked as a feast, and his name is included in Eucharistic Prayer I (The Roman Canon).

Meditation: In what ways has God multiplied your generosity?

Prayer: Ever-living God, you entrust your bountiful gifts to people that they might imitate you in giving them away to others. Make us grateful for these blessings, and, through the intercession of St. Lawrence, make us generous in good works. We ask this through our Lord Jesus Christ, your Son, who lives and reigns with you and the Holy Spirit, one God, forever and ever. Amen.

Wheat

John 12:24–26

Scripture: Jesus said, ". . . [U]nless a grain of wheat falls to the earth and dies, it remains just a single grain; but if it dies, it bears much fruit" (John 12:24).

Reflection: The pericope from John's Gospel assigned to the Feast of St. Lawrence follows Jesus' triumphant entry into Jerusalem and the request of "some Greeks" (12:20) to see Jesus. The answer that Jesus gives is addressed to Philip, who came and spoke to Andrew. The opening line of the answer is omitted by the Lectionary: "The hour has come for the Son of Man to

Feast of St. Lawrence, Deacon and Martyr

be glorified" (12:23). Up to this point in John's Gospel, the reader has been told repeatedly that Jesus' "hour" has not yet come. The word "hour" refers to his death, resurrection, and glorification. After entering Jerusalem, the Johannine Jesus, who is in charge of everything, declares that he will now die, be raised, and be glorified by God.

The passage chosen for this feast is framed by Jesus' words about his "hour." After he finishes what is today's gospel, he asks his hearers: ". . . [W]hat should I say?—'Father, save me from this hour?' No, it is for this reason that I have come to this hour" (12:27). Willingly, the Johannine Jesus accepts his death because he knows that the Father will raise him to new life.

He compares his death to that of a grain of wheat. Until the grain is planted, it remains a single grain of wheat. Once it is planted in the earth, however, it dies. The husk is softened by the rain, and the tiny plant within the seed begins to grow. Once the stalk of wheat grows, it produces fruit; it brings forth many more grains of wheat. In other words, Jesus' impending death on the cross is the means for the resurrection of all who believe in him.

The application is made even more clearly in the next verse: "Those who love their life lose it, and those who hate their life in this world will keep it for eternal life" (12:25). This life is not all there is; there is more on the other side of the grave. Being focused only on this life leaves no time to be focused on eternal life; thus, life will be lost. Being focused on eternal life leaves no time to be focused on this life; thus, life will be saved for all eternity.

Those who believe in Jesus serve him and follow him through death to resurrection and new life. Thus, where he is, his servants will be. Indeed, those who serve him are honored by the Father.

In the context of today's Feast of St. Lawrence, the gospel is meant to refer to the saint's martyrdom. As a middle-of-the-third-century deacon of Rome, Lawrence was responsible for managing the material goods of the church and distributing alms to the poor. As far as Lawrence was concerned, the real treasure of the church consisted of the widows, the poor, and the sick of Rome whom he served. When he was asked by authorities to present the church's treasure, he brought out those for whom he cared. This insult resulted in his death, which, like a grain of wheat, produced much fruit in terms of the growth of Christianity.

St. Lawrence stands as a model of what we should truly treasure. While he was entrusted with the safe-keeping of the church's material wealth, he used it to provide for the church's true wealth: the widows, the poor, the sick. As we watch the unemployment lines grow and the soup kitchen lines wind around the corner, we need more people like Lawrence to take care of the hungry, the homeless, the diseased, and the victims of natural disasters and war.

Meditation: In what ways do you imitate St. Lawrence?

Prayer: Ever-living God, you sent your Son to be like a grain of wheat that dies, grows, and produces much fruit. Through the intercession of St. Lawrence, open our eyes to see all the ways we can die to ourselves in order to give life to all who are in need. May we always treasure them as we strive to serve and follow Jesus Christ, who lives and reigns with you and the Holy Spirit, one God, forever and ever. Amen.

✣ August 24
Feast of St. Bartholomew, Apostle

Twelve

Revelation 21:9b–14

Scripture: ". . . [T]he wall of [the holy city Jerusalem coming down out of heaven from God] has twelve foundations, and on them are the twelve names of the twelve apostles of the Lamb" (Rev 21:14).

Reflection: The second to last chapter of the Book of Revelation portrays the union of heaven to earth using the wedding metaphor. John of Patmos, the author of the book, functions as seer. One of seven angels (three, signifying the spiritual order, plus four, signifying the created order) shows him "the bride, the wife of the Lamb" (21:9). On a "great, high mountain," a place of revelation and encounter with God, John sees "the holy city Jerusalem coming down out of heaven from God" (21:10). Because the city "has the glory of God" (21:11), it is God's dwelling place, like the temple of old. In other words, God is wedding heaven to earth.

In order for God's people (signified by the number twelve, which is the product of three and four) to enter the city, there are twelve gates upon which are inscribed "the names of the twelve tribes of the Israelites" (21:12), three each facing the four cardinal directions. Since God's people have been expanded by the death and resurrection of the Lamb (Jesus Christ), the city has "twelve foundations, and on them are the twelve names of the twelve apostles of the Lamb" (21:14).

The description of the city continues long after the Lectionary passage ends. However, these six verses are enough for the Feast of St. Bartholomew, one of those twelve apostles of the Lamb about whom we know little to nothing. His name appears in the gospels of Mark, Matthew, and Luke, but not in John.

So, what we celebrate today is apostleship. Even though the events of Bartholomew's life are lost in history, he, like the other apostles, was sent to proclaim the good news of the death and resurrection of Jesus Christ. As one of the twelve, his name forms the foundation of the new Jerusalem from heaven wedding the earth so that God and people are united as one.

Every time we recite the Nicene Creed, we stand on Bartholomew. We profess belief in "one, holy, catholic, and apostolic Church." The *Catechism of the Catholic Church* reminds us: "The Church is apostolic because she is founded on the apostles, in three ways: (1) she was and remains built on 'the foundation of the Apostles,' and witnesses chosen and sent on mission by Christ himself; (2) with the help of the Spirit dwelling in her, the Church keeps and hands on the teaching, the 'good deposit,' the salutary words she has heard from the apostles; (3) she continues to be taught, sanctified, and guided by the apostles until Christ's return, through their successors in pastoral office: the college of bishops, 'assisted by priests, in union with the successor of Peter, the Church's supreme pastor . . .'" (857).

Meditation: How do you experience the apostolicity of the Church?

Prayer: Father of our Lord Jesus Christ, you have wedded heaven to earth through your Son's death and resurrection. As citizens of the new Jerusalem, pour on us the same Holy Spirit that you bestowed upon St. Bartholomew that we may bear witness to the Lamb, who lives and reigns with you and the Holy Spirit, forever and ever. Amen.

Nathanael

John 1:45–51

Scripture: "Jesus answered [Nathanael], 'Do you believe because I told you that I saw you under the fig tree? You will see greater things than these'" (John 1:50).

Feast of St. Bartholomew, Apostle

Reflection: After reading today's passage from John's Gospel, the reader begins to wonder what relevance it has to the Feast of St. Bartholomew, who is mentioned in the list of apostles in the gospels of Mark, Matthew, and Luke. John's Gospel does not provide a list of twelve apostles, but the authors do mention a Nathanael, who appears after Philip is named. In the lists in the Synoptics (Mark, Matthew, and Luke), Bartholomew's name always appears after Philip's name. So, the church has concluded that Nathanael in John's Gospel is the same as Bartholomew in the Synoptic Gospels.

The pericope illustrates a process of calling disciples that is unique to the Johannine authors, namely, one disciple summons another one. For example, Andrew hears Jesus, then he finds his brother, Simon Peter, and brings him to Jesus. Likewise, after Philip has been called he finds Nathanael and invites him to follow him. Nathanael is at first reluctant, quoting an old proverb, "Can anything good come out of Nazareth?" (1:46) Philip responds, "Come and see" (1:46).

As Nathanael and Philip approach Jesus, Jesus declares that Nathanael is "truly an Israelite in whom there is no deceit!" (1:47) Nathanael is astonished that Jesus would know what an authentic Jew he is, since he has never met him. The all-knowing Jesus of John's Gospel says, "I saw you under the fig tree before Philip called you" (1:48). That's all Nathanael needs to make his profession of faith: "Rabbi, you are the Son of God! You are the King of Israel!" (1:49) In other words, Nathanael not only declares that Jesus is the Davidic Messiah, but he discloses the outline for the rest of the gospel, which will expand that vision.

Nathanael makes but one more appearance in John's Gospel, and that is the additional chapter, twenty-one, where he is listed as one of those at the Sea of Tiberias who goes fishing and to whom the resurrected Jesus makes an appearance.

In celebrating the Feast of St. Bartholomew (Nathanael) it is good to reflect upon the process illustrated by the Johannine authors, namely, one disciple summons another one. We have a tendency to leave evangelization to the professionals—priests, deacons, nuns, etc. However, every follower of Jesus is an apostle, one who is sent. A few words about the importance of participation in Sunday worship may be all that is necessary to invite another to attend a church of his or her choice on the Lord's Day. Personal witness to neighbors, such as rest on Sunday, not mowing the yard, not engaging in home-improvement projects, may be the best way to say, "Come and see!" Practicing stewardship of time, talent, treasure can bring us to others, who will see our example and want to imitate it.

Meditation: In what ways can you be a disciple who summons others?

Prayer: Heavenly Father, you sent the Son of Man to announce your gift of eternal life to the world. He called others to believe in him and you, and they, in turn, summoned others. Make of us disciples like Bartholomew (Nathanael), that we may boldly proclaim that Jesus Christ is the Son of God and the king of Israel, forever and ever. Amen.

✤August 29
Memorial of the Martyrdom of St. John the Baptist

Truth to Power

Mark 6:17–29

Scripture: "[The soldier of the guard] went off and beheaded [John the Baptist] in the prison, brought his head on a platter, and gave it to [Herodias' daughter]. Then the girl gave it to her mother [, Herodias]" (Mark 6:27–28).

Reflection: This biblical feast of the martyrdom of John the Baptist is narrated by Mark, Matthew, and Luke. Mark's account is chosen because Matthew has refashioned the story he found in Mark to make it look more like the Hebrew Bible (Old Testament) account of Ahab and Jezebel with Elijah their opponent (1 Kings 16:29–22:40); and once Luke states that Herod shut up John in prison (3:20), he condenses the account of John's beheading by omitting the flashback he found in Mark and recording only the three verses that introduce it (9:7–9).

Even though the author of Mark's Gospel refers to "King Herod" (6:14), Herod Antipas was the son of Herod the Great and tetrarch, not king, of Galilee and Perea. The author narrates the story as a flashback, an event of the past that is told in the present because it contains information that is needed by the reader. The flashback is occasioned by the rumor Herod hears: "John the Baptist has been raised from the dead; and for this reason these powers are at work in [Jesus]" (6:14). Herod states, "John whom I beheaded, has been raised" (6:16). Then the flashback begins describing the beheading of John the Baptist.

John had been arrested by Herod because he spoke against Herod's marriage to Herodias, who was married to Philip, Herod's half-brother.

According to the Torah, this is incest and forbidden (Lev 18:16; 20:21); Herodias is married to two living brothers. This is why John the Baptist told Herod, "It is not lawful for you to have your brother's wife" (6:18).

Herodias harbors a grudge against John because of his words, but she could not just outright have him killed "for Herod feared John, knowing that he was a righteous and holy man" (6:20). In fact, according to Mark, "When [Herod] heard him, he was greatly perplexed; and yet he liked to listen to him" (6:20). The Matthean Herod is more adamant about getting rid of John than the Markan Herod (Matt 14:5).

Herodias gets her chance to get rid of John on the occasion of Herod's birthday party. A girl dances for Herod and pleases him. Mark identifies her as Herod's daughter, Herodias (6:22); Matthew identifies her as "Herodias' daughter" (14:6). In later history, she is known as Salome. Whoever she was, she pleased Herod, and that prompts him to say, "Ask me for whatever you wish, and I will give it" (6:22). After conferring with her mother, she goes to Herod and says, "I want you to give me at once the head of John the Baptist on a platter" (6:25).

Now Herod is stuck between a rock and a hard place—he admires John, but he has made a promise to the dancing girl before all in attendance at his birthday party. According to Mark, "Immediately the king sent a soldier of the guard with orders to bring John's head" (6:27). The executioner does as he is told and brings the head on a platter and gives it to the girl, who, in turn, hands it to her mother.

Mark continues the story, writing, "When [John's] disciples heard about it, they came and took his body, and laid it in a tomb" (6:29). Mark includes this detail at the end of the flashback because John's beheading in the first half of Mark's Gospel is paralleled by Jesus' crucifixion in the second half of the story. John's disciples bury the body of their master; Jesus' disciples disappear from the account once he is arrested and never return. Joseph of Arimathea, who has never appeared in the gospel before this point and certainly is not one of the Twelve, suddenly comes into the narrative, gets permission from Pilate to take Jesus' dead body, wraps it in a linen shroud, and places it in a tomb.

Celebrating the memorial of the martyrdom of John the Baptist marks the death of one of the greatest men in history. Mark's Gospel is swift in its narrative about John the Baptist appearing in the wilderness, proclaiming a baptism of repentance for the forgiveness of sins, Jesus' appearance, and John's baptism of Jesus in the Jordan. All of this takes place in the first eleven verses of Mark's Gospel! John's role is simple, namely, to prepare the way for the one who will baptize with the Holy Spirit.

John's truth is further emphasized by the flashback about his death. He opposes Herod's marriage to his brother's wife. Herod knows John is right, that is, that he speaks the truth. Mark indicates that he is fascinated by what John says. However, Herod's non-repentance blinds him to the truth of the Baptist's prison ministry. By making a promise to a girl that he must keep, he ends up doing Herodias' will instead of God's will. John remains firmly planted in God's will, even when his head is removed from his body and presented to Herod on a platter.

When we stand up to power, we pay a price. It may not be martyrdom, but it will entail some kind of suffering. Those who stand up to the government and reveal to the public all the waste that goes on may not lose their jobs, but often wish that they did. Those who stand up to their boss often find themselves ignored when it is time for promotion. Being ostracized from the neighborhood often results when one calls authorities to come quiet some noise or cage a free-roaming dog. Presenting truth to power can result in the loss of one's head; ask John the Baptist.

Meditation: When have you stood up with truth to power? What were the results?

Prayer: God of John the Baptist, you filled your prophet with your Holy Spirit that he might prepare the world for the preaching of your Son. Announcing your truth brought about his death. Send us the Holy Spirit that we may not only live your word, but speak it wherever it needs to be heard. We ask this through our Lord Jesus Christ, who lives and reigns with you and the Holy Spirit, one God, forever and ever. Amen.

✤ September 8
Feast of the Nativity of the Blessed Virgin Mary

Bethlehem of Ephrathah

(1) Micah 5:1–4a (5:2–5a)

Scripture: "In that day, says the LORD, . . . [Y]ou, O Bethlehem of Ephrathah, who are one of the little clans of Judah, from you shall come forth for me one who is to rule in Israel, whose origin is from of old, from ancient days" (Mic 4:6; 5:1 [5:2]).

Reflection: The first option for the first reading on the Feast of the Nativity of the Blessed Virgin Mary is taken from the prophet Micah, but it has nothing to do with the birthday of the Virgin. The passage from Micah was written after the fall of Jerusalem to King Nebuchadnezzar of Babylon in 587 BC and the end of the Davidic dynasty.

As part of one of Micah's salvation speeches, which were added at a later date to the original book, today's pericope is addressed to the exiles in Babylon. Micah presents the hope for a restored monarchy that would come from Bethlehem, David's hometown, and from Ephrathah, David's clan. However, until "she who is in labor has brought forth" (5:2/5:3), the exiles will not be able to return to Israel.

Like David before him, Micah's hoped-for ruler will "stand and feed his flock in the strength of the LORD, in the majesty of the name of the LORD his God" (5:3/5:4). Thus, the people "shall live secure, for now he shall be great to the ends of the earth; and he shall be the one of peace" (5:3–4/5:4–5).

This passage is presented as the first option for the Feast of the Nativity of the Blessed Virgin Mary because "she who is in labor has brought forth" (5:2/5:3), that is, Mary gave birth to Jesus Christ in Bethlehem, according to Matthew's Gospel (2:1). And Jesus, "whose origin is from of old, from ancient days" (5:1/5:2), is "the Messiah, the Son of David, the Son of Abraham," according to Matthew (1:1).

While the reading is about the fruit of Mary's womb from a Christian position, the feast is the birthday of Jesus' mother, about which we know nothing. Non-biblical tradition tells us that Mary is the daughter of Joachim and Anne. However, she had to be born somewhere, but her importance comes into play only after the death and resurrection of her Son. In other words, her purpose is understood only in hindsight.

And what is true of the Blessed Virgin Mary is true of us. While we may have a birth certificate which indicates the city of our nativity, we did not know our purpose in God's plan until long after our birthday. It takes lots of discernment to understand what God is asking of us, and we often don't know exactly what it is until we reach our middle or older years. We do not have the benefit of foresight, but with hindsight we, like Mary, can see the hand of God guiding us to where the Holy One desired we be present.

Meditation: At this point in your life, what do you think God's purpose is for you?

Prayer: Father, on this birthday of the Blessed Virgin Mary we honor the mother of your Son. In your infinite wisdom you prepared her to conceive by the Holy Spirit and give birth to Jesus Christ. Help us to know our purpose in your plan that we may share in the life of him whose origin is from of old, from ancient days, the Messiah, the Son of David, who lives and reigns with you and the Holy Spirit, one God, forever and ever. Amen.

Foreknowledge

(2) Romans 8:28–30

Scripture: ". . . [T]hose whom [God] foreknew he also predestined to be conformed to the image of his Son, in order that he might be the firstborn within a large family" (Rom 8:29).

Reflection: The second option for the first reading for the Feast of the Nativity of the Blessed Virgin Mary consists of three verses which form a summary of Paul's three grounds for hope (the groaning of creation, the groaning of ourselves, the groaning of the Spirit). Because people cannot see the goal to which they are being led by God, "all things work together for good for those who love God, who are called according to his purpose" (8:28). That purpose is, of course, salvation, the full realization of God's plan through their lives.

This is an eternal, unfolding design of God in Pauline thought. The unfolding of the plan is underway, and the Blessed Virgin Mary's birth was a part of it. The divine plan leans evermore toward its goal. Because only God can know the whole of the plan, and because Paul—and, consequently, all of us—can know only those parts that have been revealed, the Apostle divides the Holy One's activity into five stages.

The first stage is God's foreknowledge. From all eternity the Divine has elected people—Jews and Gentiles—for salvation. Second, God predestined them "to be conformed to the image of his Son, in order that he might be the firstborn within a large family" (8:29). Paul does not use the word "predestination" in the same way as the Reformers did, namely as divine determination as to salvation or damnation. For Paul, predestination indicates that God wills all people to be saved. The way of salvation is participation in the life of the risen Christ so that he is the firstborn of many brothers and sisters.

Third, those whom God predestined "he also called" (8:30). The Mighty One once called a people—Hebrews, Israelites, Jews—to himself. Through the ministry of his Son, he has called Gentiles. Thus, the call has gone to all people, because God desires that all people be saved.

Fourth, those whom God called "he also justified" (8:30). God has made the first move to make it possible for people to (re-)enter a relationship with him. Through his only-begotten Son, God not only reached out to people, he showed them in human form how to respond to and cultivate a healthy relationship with God. We do not come to God on our own initiative; God first calls and then makes it possible for us to respond through grace.

Fifth, those whom God justified "he also glorified" (8:30). Here, Paul refers to the final state that the Creator intended from the beginning, namely, likeness to God. This glorification is in process, that is, it is already underway. Certainly, the Blessed Virgin Mary—conceived without original sin and raised from the dead—shares in the fullness of God's glory. We, who are in process, await this final act that occurs on the other side of death.

Celebrating the birth of the Blessed Virgin Mary offers us the opportunity to reflect upon the stages of God's plan in our lives. Her parents, Joachim and Anne, participated in God's plan. She, foreknown by God, was predestined to conceive and give birth to the Son of God. She answered the call, and God justified her. Through her assumption, the Creator glorified her. After her firstborn Son, she is the second human being to be brought to the fullness of life that God intended from the beginning.

Meditation: What did God foreknow about you? For what did God predestine you? What divine call did you answer? How did God assist you in answering his call? And in what glory of God have you already shared?

Prayer: All-knowing Father, you have predestined all people to share your eternal life. Through your Son, born of the Blessed Virgin Mary, you call them and grace them so that they can respond to you. Grant that we may share in the fullness of the glory of your Trinitarian life: Father, Son, and Holy Spirit, one God, forever and ever. Amen.

Straight Line, Crooked Lives

Matthew 1:1–16, 18–23 or 1:18–23

Scripture: "... [A]n angel of the Lord appeared to [Joseph] in a dream and said, 'Joseph, son of David, do not be afraid to take Mary as your wife, for the child conceived in her is from the Holy Spirit. She will bear a son, and you are to name him Jesus, for he will save his people from their sins'" (Matt 1:20–21).

Reflection: According to the "Protoevangelium of James," an apocryphal gospel, the parents of the Blessed Virgin Mary were Joachim and Anne, whose optional memorial is July 26. We don't know when Mary was born; this feast comes nine months after the celebration of the Solemnity of the Immaculate Conception of the Blessed Virgin Mary, December 8.

The gospel passage for this feast—all material unique to the first gospel—presents Matthean theology. The author, writing around 80 AD to a Jewish-Christian audience connects Jesus to Abraham and David through his genealogy to prove that he is the Messiah—albeit not the warrior-king for whom the Jews had hoped.

To be sure that his readers understand that Jesus is Jewish, Matthew declares that "Jesus the Messiah [is] . . . the son of Abraham" (1:1), the founder of Judaism. He also declares him to be a "son of David" (1:1), because it was from David's line that a new king was expected, and it was to David that God made the everlasting covenant that one of his descendants would sit on his throne forever. However, during the Babylonian Captivity, the Davidic lineage came to an end.

The author of this gospel conveniently groups Jesus' ancestors into three sets of fourteen generations each. Three indicates that a theophany, a manifestation of God, is occurring; this is stated more clearly later when, quoting Isaiah, Matthew declares that Jesus is called "Emmanuel, which means, 'God with us'" (1:23). This meaning of Emmanuel is confirmed by the last line Jesus says in Matthew's Gospel: "I am with you always, to the end of the age" (28:20).

The use of fourteen is the numerical value of the letters that form the name "David." Before Arabic numbers were invented, letters were used to represent numbers. The total of the letters forming the name David is fourteen. While the first two sets of ancestors contain fourteen names, the last set contains only thirteen!

Woven into Matthew's genealogy are four women. Two of them are Jewish: Tamar and Rahab. Two of them are Gentile: Ruth and Uriah's wife (Bathsheba). According to Matthew, Jesus' ancestors consist of Jews and Gentiles. This prepares the way for the Gentiles in Matthew's church; in fact, Gentiles are the heroes in Matthew's Gospel. The first to visit the child Jesus are the magi—Gentiles—from the East. Jesus declares a Roman centurion, a Gentile, to have more faith than he has found in Israel! Jesus declares a Canaanite woman, a Gentile, to have great faith after she begs him to help her daughter. Gentiles are entering Matthew's Jewish church, and he provides a precedent for them through two women in Jesus' genealogy.

The Matthean Joseph is modeled after Jacob's son, Joseph, who was a dreamer; in fact, Matthew's Joseph's father is named Jacob! For Matthew's readers, this indicates that God is rewriting history. The angel of the Lord, who guides God's people, appears to Joseph and directs him to take his

Feast of the Nativity of the Blessed Virgin Mary

pregnant fiancée as his wife. Later, Joseph is directed by God through more dreams as the rest of the unique infancy material unfolds. In Matthew's Gospel, the activity of the angel of the Lord culminates on Easter Sunday, when the angel descends from heaven, rolls back the stone from the entrance to Jesus' tomb, and declares to the women that Jesus has been raised from the dead.

Matthew declares Joseph to be a righteous man, meaning that he does the right thing because it is the right thing to do. This theme—not to mention the word "righteous"—permeates Matthew's Gospel. In order for Joseph to do the right thing, he has to break the Torah; if he followed the Torah, the usual way of being righteous, he should have had Mary stoned. And yet Matthew declares him righteous—even though he breaks Torah—because he does the right thing; he takes Mary as his wife into his house. The Matthean Jesus will develop the theme of righteousness in the Sermon on the Mount.

It does not take a rocket scientist to figure out that Matthew's genealogy is not a list of Jesus' ancestors; it is a story of how God writes straight with the crooked lives of people of the past. The genealogy ends with Joseph, who is not Jesus' father if he is conceived in his mother "from the Holy Spirit" (1:18); that is the reader's clue to look for something different in it. The incomprehensible conception of Jesus in Mary's womb by the Holy Spirit is a new example of God writing straight through the lives of crooked people, according to Matthew.

In celebrating the feast of the birthday of the Blessed Virgin Mary, we are presented the birth of her Son, Jesus. Her birthday—whenever it was—has meaning because she bore the One who saved his people from their sins. Like other famous people before her—Abraham and David, Ruth and Bathsheba—she is God's instrument. In marking this feast, we look to the one who conceived and gave birth to Jesus, Emmanuel, and wonder what God may be doing in our lives to further his plan of salvation.

Meditation: What crooked road, event, deed, etc. in your life has become a straight line for God?

Prayer: Father of our Lord Jesus Christ, you chose the Blessed Virgin Mary to be the mother of your Son. Fill us with the same Holy Spirit who brought about the conception of Jesus within her, that we may know your will and do it. May we be found worthy of the kingdom, where you live and reign as one God, forever and ever. Amen.

✤September 15
Memorial of Our Lady of Sorrows

Sorrow 1

(1) John 19:25–27

Scripture: "When Jesus saw his mother and the disciple whom he loved standing beside her, he said to his mother, 'Woman, here is your son.' Then he said to the disciple, 'Here is your mother.' And from that hour the disciple took her into his own home" (John 19:26–27).

Reflection: One option for a gospel passage proper for today's memorial of Our Lady of Sorrows is unique to John's Gospel. No other narrative portrays Jesus' mother at the foot of the cross. Likewise, no other gospel presents the account of the wedding at Cana, where the mother of Jesus makes her only other appearance in John's Gospel. The reader should conclude that these two scenes are connected, as indeed they are.

    The unnamed mother of Jesus, whom he addresses as "Woman," learns at the wedding feast that his hour has not yet come. The unnamed mother of Jesus, whom he addresses as "Woman," learns that his hour has come as he prepares for death on the cross. Thus, these two scenes serve as bookends for John's Gospel. Furthermore, his mother is entrusted to the disciple Jesus loved, another unnamed character in John's Gospel, who makes his first appearance during the supper when Jesus washes the disciples' feet, "reclining next to him" (13:23). Both his mother and the disciple Jesus loved are presented as ideal disciples in John's Gospel, because they do what he tells them.

    Mary is given the title of Our Lady of Sorrows to connect her memorial to yesterday's Feast of the Exaltation of the Holy Cross. Popular piety fixed her sorrows at seven: Simeon's declaration that her soul would be pierced with a sword in Luke's Gospel; the flight into Egypt in Matthew's Gospel; the loss of the twelve-year-old Jesus in the Temple in Luke's Gospel; the death of Joseph not recorded in any gospel; the meeting with Jesus on the way to his death not recorded in any gospel; standing at the foot of the cross in John's Gospel; and the removal of Jesus' body from the cross and its burial found in all four gospels.

The experience of sorrow is a part of life that usually follows the loss of something. When we lose a job for any reason, we are sorrowful. When a relative or friend dies, we experience sorrow. In the face of a natural disaster—flood, tornado, earthquake, etc.—we feel sorrow. In marking the memorial of Our Lady of Sorrows, we are invited to share her grief at the death of her Son. Maybe only parents, especially mothers, really know what it is like to lose a child in death. Their grief and sadness take the place of the hope they had for the future of their child. At the foot of the cross, Mary's sadness reached a crescendo as her Son entrusted his beloved mother to the care of his beloved disciple, and vice-versa. Then, he bowed his head and died. She could not have known that three days later God would raise him from the dead.

Meditation: What has been your greatest sorrow? What new life came as a result of going through it?

Prayer: Compassionate God, you heard the cries of your children and sent Jesus to save them. He demonstrated your compassion from the cross, entrusting his mother to his beloved disciple. As we celebrate this memorial of Our Lady of Sorrows, fill us with your Holy Spirit of compassion that we may share in the suffering and death of your Son with the hope of rising with him to new life. We ask this in the name of Jesus, the Lord. Amen.

Sorrow 2

(2) Luke 2:33–35

Scripture: "... Simeon ... said to [Jesus'] mother, Mary, '... [A] sword will pierce your own soul ...'" (Luke 2:34–35).

Memorial of Our Lady of Sorrows

Reflection: Mary is given the title Our Lady of Sorrows to connect this memorial to yesterday's Feast of the Exaltation of the Holy Cross. Popular piety fixed her sorrows at seven. The first is found in today's second option for a proper gospel for this memorial. Simeon, a character unique to Luke's Gospel, is present when Jesus' parents bring the child to Jerusalem to present him to the Lord in the Temple. After taking the child in his arms, Simeon praises God for the salvation the child brings. Then, he declares that Mary's soul will be pierced with a sword.

The other six sorrows of the Blessed Virgin Mary include the flight into Egypt in Matthew's Gospel; the loss of the twelve-year-old Jesus in the Temple in Luke's Gospel; the death of Joseph not recorded in any gospel; the meeting with Jesus on the way to his death not recorded in any gospel; standing at the foot of the cross in John's Gospel; and the removal of Jesus' body from the cross and its burial found in all four gospels.

The context for this optional proper gospel illustrates several important Lukan themes. The account of the presentation in the Temple is one of a pair of Jesus' childhood stories in Luke's Gospel—the other is the loss of the twelve-year-old Jesus in the Jerusalem Temple after the feast of Passover. The young Jesus, who is presented to God and redeemed, is the redeemer of the world. Once he is found in the Temple, he declares that he has been about his Father's business.

The author of Luke's Gospel likes using hymns in his narrative. When Mary visits Elizabeth, she breaks out into song. After John the Baptist is born, Zechariah sings a hymn. Angels chant a song after Jesus is born. And once Simeon recognizes the Messiah, he, too, sings a song. The songs serve as summaries of Lukan theology: God has brought salvation for Jews and Gentiles.

Luke likes to parallel a story about a man with one about a woman. Thus, Simeon is paired with the prophetess Anna in the account of the presentation. Before this, Mary's parallel is found in Zechariah—both of them are visited by the angel Gabriel.

Today's memorial focuses on Simeon's words to Jesus' parents, namely, that he will be the vehicle for the fall and rise of many in Israel, and that he will be a sign that is opposed. This summary of Luke's Gospel and his second volume, the Acts of the Apostles, paves the way for God's initiative or plan to save both Jews and Gentiles. As God's plan is put into action, "the inner thoughts of many will be revealed" (2:35). God's plan will provoke change, suffering, and some will not be able to change, while others will greet it with open arms.

According to Simeon's words, Mary herself will be confronted with change, which will result in suffering. Such is the case when she and Jesus' brothers arrive where he is, but cannot get near him; he declares that his mother and brothers "are those who hear the word of God and do it" (8:21). After teaching about unclean spirits, a woman in the crowd praises the womb that bore him and the breasts that nursed him, that is, his mother. He replies, "Blessed . . . are those who hear the word of God and obey it!" (11:28) And, of course, there is the suffering she endures when her only-begotten Son is crucified.

But the suffering she endured did not dampen her faith. In the Acts of the Apostles, she is named among those who were "constantly devoting themselves to prayer" (1:14). Change brings about suffering, and suffering can deepen trust in God. The sorrows of the Blessed Virgin Mary attest to this truth. And if we examine our lives carefully, we discover the same.

The change in diet required to lose weight or to lower cholesterol will cause suffering; having faith in the results that the diet will bring often leads to a healthier life. Those with cancer know the suffering associated with radiation therapy and chemotherapy, but the suffering often sparks a deeper trust of God and brings about a longer life. Even a move—from one town to another or from one home to another—is a change filled with suffering for the whole family. But once all are settled and reflect upon the past, they might begin to see how God was leading them to the new place. The mother of Jesus learned that change leads to suffering, and suffering leads to deeper faith in God and his plan for the salvation of the world.

Meditation: What recent change resulted in suffering and a deeper faith in God for you?

Prayer: To the Virgin Mary of Nazareth, O God, you made known your plan to save the world. She willingly cooperated with you in giving birth to your Son, Jesus, who brought about change, suffering, and a renewed faith in you, his Father. Guide us through change and suffering with the Holy Spirit that our trust may deepen in your Trinitarian life: Father, Son, and Holy Spirit, one God, forever and ever. Amen.

✤ September 21
Feast of St. Matthew, Apostle and Evangelist

Maturity in Faith

Ephesians 4:1–7, 11–13

Scripture: "The gifts [Christ] gave were that some would be apostles, some prophets, some evangelists, some pastors and teachers, to equip the saints for the work of ministry, for building up the body of Christ, until all of us come to the unity of faith and of the knowledge of the Son of God, to maturity, to the measure of the full stature of Christ" (Eph 4:11–13).

Reflection: The letter to the Ephesians, written by a follower of Paul around 80 AD, places an emphasis on maintaining "the unity of the Spirit in the bond of peace" (4:3). The passage assigned for the Feast of St. Matthew, Apostle and Evangelist, references both apostles and evangelists in its list of gifts that are given to maintain the "one body and one Spirit, . . . the one hope . . . , one Lord, one faith, one baptism" (4:4–5). The reason the post-Pauline author gives for leading "a life worthy of the calling to which [the Ephesians] have been called" (4:1) is in imitation of the "one God and Father of all, who is above all and through all and in all" (4:6).

The Pauline concept of the body of Christ is expanded by the letter to the Ephesians. Paul's original concept of one body with many members, each using his or her gift to keep the body functioning, takes on cosmic proportions in Ephesians. The various gifts given to people have a specific purpose: "to equip the saints for the work of ministry, for building up the body of Christ, until all of us come to the unity of faith and of the knowledge of the Son of God, to maturity, to the measure of the full stature of Christ" (4:12–13). This long sentence needs to be unpacked.

The saints are believers, who are to serve each other. In the very act of serving each other as preachers of the gospel, as ministers of social justice, as shepherds of the flock, as catechists of the faith, they help to build the one body of Christ. The result of this building "with all humility and gentleness, with patience, bearing with one another in love" (4:2) is the coming of all people to the unity of faith and knowing the Son of God. The post-Pauline author understands that once all believe, the result with be a maturity. The full stature of Christ will be reached.

Needless to say, we are far from the post-Pauline ideal. We live in a culture that promotes the use of individual gifts for the acquisition of wealth—not always for the common good. Many people never reach adult maturity even though they reach the fullness of years; they never take responsibility for themselves, always blaming others for their mistakes and, when they do not get their way, like children they take their toys and go home. Individual likes and dislikes, impatience, rumors, etc. fragment the unity the Ephesians' author so strongly desired. Helping, coaxing, challenging growth to adult wholeness in Christ remains both a task and a hope for the future. The task is to change the perspective from the individual to the common good. Only by teaching believers to place the common good ahead of their individual goods can the body of Christ reach its full stature. So, on this Feast of St. Matthew, whose gospel attempts to hold together one church composed of Jews and Gentiles, we are left with the hope for adult maturity in the one faith.

Meditation: What gets in your way of reaching adult maturity in Christ?

Prayer: Almighty God, you are the one Father of all, and you desire that your people become one body and one Spirit in your Son, Jesus Christ. As we celebrate the feast of St. Matthew, open our minds and hearts to understand the calling we have received to be one in hope, one in faith, and one in baptism, that we may use your gifts to the measure of the full stature of Christ, who lives and reigns with you and the Holy Spirit, one God, forever and ever. Amen.

Feast of St. Matthew, Apostle and Evangelist

Tax Collector

Matthew 9:9-13

Scripture: "As Jesus was walking along, he saw a man named Matthew sitting at the tax booth; and he said to him, 'Follow me!' And he got up and followed him" (Matt 9:9).

Reflection: Only in Matthew's Gospel is the tax collector named Matthew; in Mark and Luke he is named Levi. This is why today's feast of St. Matthew, apostle and evangelist, is assigned this pericope. We do not know who wrote Matthew's Gospel, since gospels are not given names until late in the second century AD.

Matthew, whose name means "gift of God," is a tax collector; the meaning of the name and the job could not be any more opposed! A tax collector was a Jew who worked for the Roman occupation forces. He made his living by raising the set amount of the Roman tax and pocketing the difference. It mattered not to the Romans how much he raised taxes; all that mattered to them was that they got what was levied. To the Jews, a tax collector was an apostate; he had renounced his faith in order to make a living, and he was a collaborator with the enemy.

The Matthean Jesus seems to draw tax collectors and sinners, those who deliberately disobey divine commands, to his company. After calling Matthew to follow him, Jesus is found at table with "many tax collectors and sinners" (9:10). It is important for the reader to know that "sinners" is a euphemism for "prostitutes." The incomprehensibility of Jesus' eating with tax collectors and sinners—indicating some affinity with them—is not lost on the stereotyped Pharisees, who ask his disciples, "Why does your teacher eat with tax collectors and sinners?" (9:11)

Jesus overhears the question and quotes an old Greek proverb: "Those who are well have no need of a physician, but those who are sick" do (9:12). In other words, tax collectors and sinners are sick, and Jesus is the divine physician who will cure them. The Pharisees consider themselves healthy, because they keep the Torah. As the Matthean Jesus makes clear, he did not come to call the righteous, but sinners. The Pharisees are sent to learn the meaning of "I desire mercy and not sacrifice" (9:13) from the prophet Hosea (6:6), indicating that while sacrifice has some value, it is meaningless without the mercy Jesus shows to repentant tax collectors and sinners.

Throughout Matthew's Gospel, Jesus proposes what biblical scholars refer to as a higher righteousness. Summarized as doing the right thing because it is the right thing to do, this higher righteousness demonstrates mercy. It is best illustrated by those who feed the hungry, give drink to the thirsty, welcome the stranger, clothe the naked, care for the sick, visit the imprisoned—and welcome tax collectors and sinners and eat with them.

In marking this feast of St. Matthew, apostle and evangelist, we do well to evaluate how well we imitate Jesus. Tax collectors and sinners do not carry the same social stigma today that they did in Jesus' day. However, we have modern tax collectors and sinners—such as the richest people in the world, those with children out of wedlock with multiple fathers, drug dealers, car and home repossessors, managers who lay off employees, etc. These are the sick people who need the divine physician, Jesus, and we, his followers, have been given the gospel to bring to them. Through our way of life, through our conversation, through our discipleship, we call them to join the ranks of fellow tax collectors and sinners.

Meditation: In what specific ways do you offer the gospel to tax collectors and sinners?

Prayer: Heavenly Father, your son, Jesus, called Matthew the tax collector to follow him, and he responded with a conversion that affected other tax collectors and sinners. Give us the courage to proclaim and to live Christ's gospel, that, through your mercy, many may be brought to discipleship. We ask this through our Lord Jesus Christ, who lives and reigns with you and the Holy Spirit, one God, forever and ever. Amen.

✤September 29
Feast of Sts. Michael, Gabriel, and Raphael, Archangels

Function

(1) Daniel 7:9–10, 13–14

Scripture: "A thousand thousands served [an Ancient One], and ten thousand times ten thousand stood attending him" (Dan 7:10).

Reflection: The first option for a first reading on the Feast of the Archangels is taken from the Book of the Prophet Daniel. More specifically, it comes from a section of the book written in the mid-second century BC to support the Maccabean revolt against the Seleucid rulers of what had once been the kingdoms of Israel and Judah. The visionary predicts a time when the Seleucids will fall and a new Jewish state will be born with its capitol at Jerusalem.

Once the Seleucid empire falls, Daniel narrates a scene that depicts the divine court. An Ancient One, probably God, takes his throne. He is dressed in snow-white clothing; his hair is like pure-white wool; flames of fire flash from his throne. The author of Daniel presents a composite of God that is drawn from 1 Kings 22, Isaiah 6, Ezekiel 1, Psalm 82, and Job 1 to indicate that God again rules his people. Daniel writes, "The court sat in judgment, and the books were opened" (7:10). The two verses of judgment upon the Seleucid rulers are omitted from today's passage.

Daniel sees "one like a human being coming with the clouds of heaven" (7:13). While in the synoptic gospels Christianity will equate this son of man with Jesus Christ, here he is the new Davidic ruler of Israel and Judah. He is presented to God and given "dominion and glory and kingship . . .

that shall never be destroyed" (7:14). In other words, this new king will establish a dynasty that will rule the whole world for ever.

This passage is chosen as the first option on the Feast of Sts. Michael, Gabriel, and Raphael because it mentions that "a thousand thousands served [an Ancient One], and ten thousand times ten thousand stood attending him" (7:10). These thousands of attendants are considered to be angels, messengers, manifestations of God serving himself. In Christian tradition, three of these manifestations are named archangels because they have a more important function.

Thus, Michael, whose name means "who is like God," and Gabriel, whose name means "the strength of God," and Raphael, whose name means "God's remedy," have specific functions. Michael is a manifestation of God's power to his people; Gabriel manifests God's strength to his people; and Raphael manifests God's healing of his people. An unkind history has taken these functions and frozen them in marble, granite, and plaster in the likeness of young men or women with flowing robes and wings sprouting from their shoulders!

Celebrating the Feast of the Archangels is not about that. Today's feast focuses on God and the many ways he reveals himself to people. He presents himself in power, in strength, and in healing. He is available in power when we do good deeds to those around us. He gives us strength to defend our faith when others would back down. And he heals our medical, psychological, and spiritual ills. When we experience God's power, strength, and healing in our lives, we have witnessed the manifestation of an archangel.

Meditation: Identify specific experiences that you have had of God's power, strength, and healing.

Prayer: Ancient One, you reveal your power, strength, and healing to your people so that they may recognize your goodness and never cease to praise you. As we mark the Feast of the Archangels Michael, Gabriel, and Raphael, pour on us the power, strength, and healing of the Holy Spirit, that we may praise you through your Son, Jesus Christ, who lives and reigns with you and the Holy Spirit, one God, forever and ever. Amen.

Feast of Sts. Michael, Gabriel, and Raphael, Archangels

God's Power

(2) Revelation 12:7–12ab

Scripture: ". . . [W]ar broke out in heaven; Michael and his angels fought against the dragon, but they were defeated, and there was no longer any place for them in heaven" (Rev 12:7–8).

Reflection: The second option for a first reading for the Feast of Michael, Gabriel, and Raphael is a passage about the defeat of evil from the Book of Revelation. More specifically, chapter 12, out of which this pericope is taken, begins the last of three stories found in this work. The setting is earth; Jesus is portrayed as the divine warrior who has come to restore all things.

After the woman gives birth to the child, who is taken to God, and she flees into the wilderness to escape the great red dragon, holy war breaks out in heaven. God, manifest as Michael (whose name means "who is like God"), defeats the dragon and tosses him out of the top story of the universe to the second story, earth. Just to be sure the reader knows who the dragon is, John of Patmos states "that ancient serpent, who is called the Devil and Satan, the deceiver of the whole world—he was thrown down to the earth" (12:9)—where he has already been defeated by "the blood of the Lamb and by the word of [the faithful's] testimony" (12:11), that is, their own martyrdom, "for they did not cling to life even in the face of death" (12:11).

God's defeat of the dragon, manifest as Michael, sparks a heavenly chorus, which announces that salvation and power and the kingdom of God and the authority of his Messiah have arrived. However, only the battle has been won in heaven; the rest of the war remains to be waged on earth.

This passage from the Book of Revelation is offered as a first reading because it mentions the name "Michael," who in the Book of Daniel is known as "the great prince, the protector of [the] people" (12:1). It is God who protects his people, of course. In the past, he protected them from slavery, from pharaoh's army, from thirst, from hunger, from enemies. In the fullness of time, he protected them from defeat with the gift of his own Son. And the Holy One continues to protect his people today from accidents, natural disasters, and, diseases. Whenever one experiences God's protection, a Michael is present—although he may be known by another name.

Meditation: In what specific ways have you experienced God's protection?

Prayer: Almighty God, you have defeated evil through the ministry of your Messiah, Jesus Christ, and those who believe in him continue to experience your protection. As we celebrate this feast in honor of your archangels, Michael, Gabriel, and Raphael, make us aware of your great gift. We praise you, Father, Son, and Holy Spirit, now and forever and ever. Amen.

Connection

John 1:47–51

Scripture: Jesus said to Nathanael, "Very truly, I tell you, you will see heaven opened and the angels of God ascending and descending upon the Son of Man" (John 1:51).

Reflection: The pericope chosen from John's Gospel for the Feast of the Archangels, Michael, Gabriel, and Raphael, alludes to three other Scripture passages. The first one is obviously Genesis 28:12, which narrates the patriarch Jacob's dream of a ladder stretching between heaven and earth with God's angels ascending and descending on it. Then, the LORD appears to Jacob and repeats the promise of land and offspring he made to Abraham, Jacob's grandfather, and Isaac, Jacob's father.

The second biblical passage to which today's gospel alludes is Daniel 7:9–14. The prophet has a vision of a throne upon which the Ancient One, God, takes his place. A thousand thousands, angels, minister to him; ten thousand times ten thousand angels stand to attend him. A Son of Man, the Messiah—later identified with Jesus—comes to the Ancient One, who gives him dominion and glory and kingship. Upon him the angels converge.

The third allusion is found within John's Gospel itself. Near the end of a lengthy dialogue with Nicodemus, Jesus tells him, "No one has ascended into heaven except the one who descended from heaven, the Son of Man" (3:13). Jesus, the Word-made flesh who has come to live among people, will be lifted up in glory on the cross.

Feast of Sts. Michael, Gabriel, and Raphael, Archangels

The allusions to biblical passages helps us to understand the Johannine point of view. God has connected heaven and earth. We must remember that ancient people lived in a three-storied universe. God lived above the dome of the sky in the heavens; people lived on the flat, plate-like surface of the earth; and the dead lived under the earth. Jacob's ladder brings together heaven and earth. Daniel's vision brings together heaven and earth. In his own person, Jesus brings together heaven and earth.

Before Jesus, angels were considered to be invisible creatures that could travel between heaven and earth. An unkind history has turned the invisible into visible winged men or women with white garments. Such iconography, however, does an injustice to the concept of angel as God's messenger uniting heaven and earth.

The feast of the archangels celebrates special occasions when God united heaven and earth. Gabriel is sent to Mary to tell her that she has been chosen to be the agent of God uniting heaven and earth in the person of the child she will conceive through the overshadowing of the Holy Spirit. Michael in heaven serves as Israel's protector on earth. And Raphael, a heavenly guide, assists all those on pilgrimage on earth. While we cannot see angels, we know that God has united heaven and earth, and God's invisible servants bring us the Holy One's greetings, they protect us from harm, and they accompany us throughout our lifetime journey on earth to the heavenly place God has prepared for us.

Meditation: In what ways have you experienced the union of heaven and earth through the medium of an (arch)angel?

Prayer: Father almighty, you are the maker of heaven and earth, of all things visible and invisible. Send your angels to protect and guide us. Grant that we may hear the message they bring from you to us, that we may praise you in the Holy Spirit and through your Son, our Lord Jesus Christ, who live and reign with you, one God, forever and ever. Amen.

✤ October 18
Feast of St. Luke, Evangelist

Luke

2 Timothy 4:10–17b

Scripture: "Only Luke is with me [, Paul]" (2 Tim 4:11a).

Reflection: Known as one of the pastoral letters, the second letter of Paul to Timothy is a second-generation Pauline creation, meaning that someone wrote it in Paul's name to address issues that had emerged near the end of the first century AD in a manner the author imagined Paul would if he were still alive. By putting Paul's name on the letter, the author gives his instruction authority that it probably would not have had.

Today's pericope is taken from near the end of the letter. It is chosen as the first reading for this Feast of St. Luke because it mentions the name Luke along with other names of teachers that appear in other mostly non-Pauline letters, specifically, Colossians, Ephesians, and Titus. Luke is one of several Latin names used extensively in the Roman Empire, so the Luke mentioned here may or may not be the same Luke who wrote the Gospel According to Luke and the Acts of the Apostles.

The writer explains to where various teachers have scattered along with a certain "Alexander the coppersmith" who opposed the preaching of the gospel. There is also a reference to no one coming to Paul's defense. The heart of this section of the closing exhortation is the author's statement: ". . . [T]he Lord stood by me [, Paul,] and gave me strength, so that through me the message might be fully proclaimed and all the Gentiles might hear it" (4:17a). Thus, we have the second reason this passage is chosen for the Feast of St. Luke, whose gospel was written primarily for Gentiles.

Luke's audience consists of upper class, rich, city-dwelling Gentiles. In his gospel, Luke demonstrates how Christianity emerges out of Judaism. By the time he writes in 90 AD Jewish Christianity is fading away and Gentile Christianity is blossoming, as seen in the Acts of the Apostles. While usually not phrased in this way, today's Christianity is Gentile, and the mission to the Gentiles continues.

Just as the author of second Timothy narrates how the teachers or catechists spread around the known world, we are urged to be like Paul and continue trusting that God will strengthen us so that through us "the message might be fully proclaimed and all the Gentiles might hear it" (4:17). In the face of opposition of any kind, we may feel like giving up, but we don't. We derive hope from "the books and . . . the parchments" (4:13), like this letter, as we continue the mission from one generation to the next.

Meditation: In what specific ways do you proclaim the message to fellow Gentiles?

Prayer: Heavenly Father, you entrusted the message of the death and resurrection of your Son to the skillful pen of Luke, one of your evangelists. Through the Holy Spirit, strengthen our understanding of his gospel and enable us to proclaim it throughout the world. All glory is yours with our Lord Jesus Christ in the unity of the Holy Spirit, forever and ever. Amen.

Kingdom of God

Luke 10:1–9

Scripture: ". . . [T]he Lord appointed seventy others and sent them on ahead of him in pairs to every town and place where he himself intended to go" (Luke 10:1).

Reflection: The gospel pericope for the Feast of St. Luke is unique to Luke's Gospel. Jesus, who is often referred to as "the Lord" in Luke's Gospel, appoints seventy or seventy-two—there are variants as to the number—and sends them out in missionary pairs. As he has done for many of his other accounts, the author of Luke's Gospel employs a Hebrew Bible (Old Testament) model.

Both the Book of Exodus (24:1, 9) and the Book of Numbers (11:16, 24–30) record an account of Moses choosing seventy elders. However, in both accounts there are also present two other men— Nadab and Abihu in Exodus, and Eldad and Medad in Numbers—who do not go with the seventy but receive the spirit of prophecy. Thus, depending on how one counts, there were seventy or seventy-two.

Seventy-two is also considered the number of the nations of the world in Genesis 10:1–32. After narrating the story of the great flood, the writer lists the descendants of Noah's three sons by family, language, land, and nation. The total number of generations is seventy-two. Since Luke is interested in portraying the Jewish Jesus' mission to the Gentiles, that is, the nations of the world, in sending out seventy(-two) he is sending out laborers to gather in the Gentile harvest. This theme is presented again in the Acts of the Apostles, Luke's volume two, which portrays Peter inaugurating the mission to the Gentiles and Paul taking over until the good news reaches the ends of the earth.

The seventy(-two) will be "like lambs in the midst of wolves" (10:3); they will be vulnerable. Thus, they are to stay focused on their task by carrying "no purse, no bag, no sandals" (10:4) and not greeting anyone along the way. They are to be peace-wishing travelers, staying in whatever home welcomes them and eating and drinking what is offered to them "for the laborer deserves to be paid" (10:7). Like Jesus, they eat whatever is set before them, they heal the sick, and they preach: "The kingdom of God has come near to you" (10:9).

Their basic message that God's kingdom is being manifest is the same as Jesus' preaching. Both the narrator of Luke's Gospel and the Lukan Jesus speaks often about the kingdom of God (4:43, 8:1, 9:2, 9:11, 11:20, 13:28–29, 21:31). However, Jesus uniquely declares, ". . . [T]he kingdom of God is among you" (17:21). Jesus' disciples are given the secrets of the kingdom of God, especially as these are revealed through parables (8:10, 13:18, 13:20). There is an urgency to make the proclamation about the kingdom of God (9:60, 9:62). Jesus heals and casts out demons as a demonstration that the kingdom of God has come (11:20), yet it is not observable (17:20), but there are signs that it is near (21:31). It must be received as a little child would accept it (18:16–17), and it is hard for those with wealth to enter it (18:24–25).

Feast of St. Luke, Evangelist

In celebrating this Feast of St. Luke, evangelist, we find ourselves immersed in the good news of Luke's Gospel, more specifically, that God's rule or reign is here. God's kingdom does not coerce people; those who preach about it invite Gentiles, the peoples of the nations of the world, to enter it and accept God as their king. We proclaim the kingdom of God in simple acts of honesty, like telling all of the truth, returning borrowed items, paying debts. We bring the kingdom to the sick in their homes, in hospitals, and in nursing homes. We demonstrate the presence of God's kingdom through our respect for the unborn, the homeless, the jobless, and the dying. If we choose to use words, the message is simple: The kingdom of God is among us. In these and in many other ways we evangelize, spread the good news, just like Luke did in writing his gospel.

Meditation: In what ways do you proclaim the kingdom of God?

Prayer: Almighty God, your Son recognized that the harvest is plentiful, but the laborers are few. Send us as laborers into your harvest. Through the Holy Spirit, give us words and deeds to proclaim the nearness of the kingdom, where you live with Jesus Christ, our Lord, and the Holy Spirit, one God, forever and ever. Amen.

✥ October 28
Feast of Sts. Simon and Jude, Apostles

Metaphors

Ephesians 2:19–22

Scripture: ". . . [Y]ou are citizens with the saints and also members of the household of God, built upon the foundation of the apostles and prophets, with Christ Jesus himself as the cornerstone" (Eph 2:19–20).

Reflection: In the second generation Pauline document known as the letter of Paul to the Ephesians, the author employs three metaphors successively: citizenship, household, and building-temple. Let's explore these.

The first metaphor is citizenship. Those who believe that Jesus died and God raised him from the dead "are no longer strangers and aliens" (2:19). Now they have a country, or they possess dual citizenship. Christ Jesus has reconciled all people—Jews and Gentiles—into one body, making them citizens of God's kingdom.

Because all people have been offered the opportunity to be citizens of God's kingdom, they can also be considered as brothers and sisters of one family in the household of God. In this second metaphor, a patriarchal family is envisioned, living in one home governed by the Father of the one family, God.

The third metaphor is the reason this passage is read on the Feast of Sts. Simon and Jude, apostles. The apostles and prophets form a foundation for the building. Christ Jesus is the cornerstone through whom "the whole structure is joined together and grows into a holy temple in the Lord" (2:21). God dwells in this building-temple.

Because we live in countries with borders protected from illegal aliens, Ephesians' vision of believers as citizens of the world can be blurred easily.

Feast of Sts. Simon and Jude, Apostles

We are members of the universal church. We profess this faith in the Nicene Creed, saying, "I believe in one, holy, catholic, and apostolic Church." We profess this faith in the Apostles' Creed, declaring, "I believe in . . . the holy Catholic Church . . . ."

The *Catechism of the Catholic Church* tells us that the church is catholic or universal in two ways. "First, the Church is catholic because Christ is present in her. In her subsists the fullness of Christ's body united with its head" (830). "Secondly, the Church is catholic because she has been sent out by Christ on a mission to the whole of the human race" (831). All people are called to belong to this one, holy, apostolic church. "The character of universality . . . is a gift from the Lord himself whereby the Catholic Church ceaselessly and efficaciously seeks for the return of all humanity and all its good, under Christ the Head in the unity of his Spirit" (831). Thus, we are catholic citizens, members of God's one family, built as a single temple in which God's Spirit dwells.

We do not need communion cards or congregational membership identity cards. No matter where we are in the universe, we have a bishop who is in union with one pope. We celebrate the Eucharist and other sacraments not as citizens of the United States or Canada or Mexico or Spain, but as members of one church, one temple fitted together by Christ in whom God dwells.

Meditation: In what ways do you participate in the universality of the church?

Prayer: God of Sts. Simon and Jude, upon your Son's apostles you have established a foundation for the temple of your dwelling. Give us a greater appreciation for the baptism that initiates us into citizenship in your kingdom. Assist us to grow in unity as members of your family. And grow us into the unity you share in Trinity: Father, Son, and Holy Spirit, one God, forever and ever. Amen.

Sent

Luke 6:12–16

Scripture: ". . . [W]hen day came, [Jesus] called his disciples and chose twelve of them, whom he also named apostles: . . . Simon, who was called the Zealot, and Judas son of James . . ." (Luke 6:13, 15–16).

Reflection: On the Feast of the Apostles Simon and Jude, the gospel passage presents Luke's list of the twelve apostles. While there are variations of the names of the twelve apostles in the gospels of Mark, Matthew, Luke, and the Acts of the Apostles—not to mention the fact that both Paul and Barnabas are called apostles in the Acts of the Apostles—Luke's narrative is chosen because it is the only list that contains an apostle named "Judas son of James" (6:16; Acts 1:13). In Mark's and Matthew's list, there is an apostle named Thaddeus (Mark 3:18, Matt 10:3), but not one named Judas son of James, and Simon is identified as the Cananean (Mark 3:18, Matt 10:4), not as the Zealot (6:15, Acts1:13).

For the author of Luke's Gospel, the choice of twelve signifies that a restored Israel is in process. In Lukan understanding, the old Israel (the Jews, represented by the twelve tribes of Israel) gives way to the new Israel (the Gentiles, represented by the twelve apostles, and Paul in the Acts). The leaders of the new Israel and their successors will bring the gospel to the nations of the world.

The apostles do this only after spending time in prayer. Before making any major decision, Luke portrays Jesus as praying. Before choosing twelve apostles, Luke narrates that Jesus "went out to the mountain to pray; and he spent the night in prayer to God" (6:12). We know that the apostles learned the importance of prayer from the example and teaching of Jesus, because in the Acts of the Apostles, Luke writes that all "were constantly devoting themselves to prayer" (1:14).

Marking the Feast of Sts. Simon and Jude reminds us that we are sent with the gospel to the nations. We bring it through our lifestyle to our workplace, to the fitness center, to the bank, to the grocery store, etc. Often, the best preaching is done in silence, that is, through behavior. Being bearers of the gospel means we are grounded in prayer, the source of our strength for continuing to carry the gospel, wherever we go. We know nothing about Simon and Jude, except that they were sent with the good news after spending time in prayer. That alone is worthy of our imitation.

Meditation: In what ways does prayer enable you to live and proclaim the gospel?

Feast of Sts. Simon and Jude, Apostles

Prayer: Ever-living God, the twelve apostles chosen by your Son were sent with the gospel to the nations. On the day of our baptism we received our calling to live the good news. Ground us in prayer and fill us with the strength of the Holy Spirit that we may be gospel heralds wherever we go. We ask this through our Lord Jesus Christ, your Son, who lives and reigns with you and the Holy Spirit, one God, forever and ever. Amen.

✠ November 18
Optional Memorial of the Dedication of the Basilica of Sts. Peter and Paul, Apostles

Unhindered Gospel

Acts 28:11–16, 30–31

Scripture: "When we came into Rome, Paul was allowed to live by himself, with the soldier who was guarding him. He lived there two whole years at his own expense and welcomed all who came to him, proclaiming the kingdom of God and teaching about the Lord Jesus Christ with all boldness and without hindrance" (Acts 28:16, 30–31).

Reflection: St. Peter Basilica was dedicated by Pope Urban VIII on November 18, 1626, and the Basilica of St. Paul Outside-the-Walls was dedicated by Pope Pius IX on December 10, 1854, but this anniversary of the dedication of earlier churches—the previous St. Peter Basilica was replaced with the current one and fire destroyed St. Paul Basilica—has been observed in Rome since the eleventh century. In the universal liturgical calendar, this is an optional memorial; if one chooses to observe it, it has proper readings that must be used.

    The edited passage from the Acts of the Apostles is composed of verses that narrate Paul's arrival in Rome and his stay there for two years under house arrest. Luke, the author of the Acts of the Apostles, which serves as the second volume of Luke's Gospel, portrays Paul as one of two heroes—the other being Peter. Paul is the apostle to the Gentiles, just like Peter is the apostle to the Jews. In the Acts, whatever one does—heal, give a speech, raise the dead—the other does as well.

    Luke does not narrate the traditional martyrdom—beheading—of Paul. He ends his second volume with Paul in Rome in his own lodgings,

Optional Memorial of the Dedication of the Basilica of Sts. Peter and Paul, Apostles

receiving all who come to him, preaching the Kingdom of God, and teaching about Jesus Christ, openly and unhindered. Luke does not want to end his two-volume work on the negative note of Paul's death; rather, he wants to end it with one of his favorite lines: The word of God continued to spread. For the same reason, the death of Peter is not narrated in the Acts of the Apostles; he simply disappears from the narrative.

The unique Lukan theme of Jesus being "a light for revelation to the Gentiles" (Luke 2:32) so that all flesh can "see the salvation of God" (3:6) is realized at the end of the Acts of the Apostles. Although the verse is not included in today's pericope, as the third to last verse of the Acts, it portrays Paul, the apostle to the Gentiles, as restating the theme: "This salvation of God has been sent to the Gentiles" (28:28). Since chapter ten of the Acts of the Apostles, Paul has been ministering to the Gentiles. Now at the end of the Acts, the gospel has been brought to the known world, openly and unhindered.

In the context of the Optional Memorial of the Dedication of the Basilica of Sts. Peter and Paul, Apostles, the passage explains how Paul got to Rome and why a church was built to commemorate his martyrdom by beheading. While we no longer live in a world that from a Jewish perspective divided people into Jews or Gentiles, we do well to reflect on our own missionary commission that occurred on the day of our baptism. While the focus of the Rite of Baptism is on the parents of the child being baptized and their responsibility to form their child in the practice of the faith, the child, nevertheless, is commissioned for mission. This commissioning is revisited during preparation for first Penance and first Eucharist and Confirmation. Hopefully, by the time he or she reaches the teenage years, the person is living and engaging in the mission to preach the kingdom of God and to teach about the Lord Jesus Christ.

Through the waters of baptism, all of us share in this mission. We preach about the kingdom of God mainly through the way we live our lives. We indicate the importance of the kingdom through simplicity of life. Instead of the largest home, we choose to live in a small one in order to save energy and serve the poor. Instead of having an acre of yard to mow, we choose a lot with only a fraction of an acre, and use the rest of our time preparing to teach in our parish school of religion. Instead of paying rent on a storage facility to keep all the stuff we own, we sell the stuff and send the proceeds to an organization that relieves hunger around the globe.

The anniversary of the dedication of a church presents us with the opportunity to remember that we are the church, that we are dedicated to God's service, that we follow in the footsteps of Jesus, that we teach about the Lord Jesus Christ, openly and unhindered, like Paul.

Meditation: In what specific ways do you fulfill your baptismal mission by the way you live your life?

Prayer: Father of all, you called Paul to be your apostle to the Gentiles, to proclaim your kingdom and to teach about your Son, our Lord Jesus Christ. Fill us, your church, with his spirit that we may bring your word to all we meet. We ask this through our Lord Jesus Christ, your Son, who lives and reigns with you and the Holy Spirit, one God, forever and ever. Amen.

Fear

Matthew 14:22-33

Scripture: ". . . [E]arly in the morning [Jesus] came walking toward [his disciples in a boat] on the sea. But when the disciples saw him walking on the sea, they were terrified, saying, 'It is a ghost!' And they cried out in fear. But immediately Jesus spoke to them and said, 'Take heart, it is I; do not be afraid.' Peter answered him, 'Lord, if it is you, command me to come to you on the water.' He said, 'Come!' So Peter got out of the boat, started walking on the water, and came toward Jesus. But when he noticed the strong wind, he became frightened, and beginning to sink, he cried out, 'Lord, save me!'" (Matt 14:25-30)

Reflection: St. Peter Basilica was dedicated by Pope Urban VIII on November 18, 1626, and the Basilica of St. Paul Outside-the-Walls was dedicated by Pope Pius IX on December 10, 1854, but this anniversary of the dedication of earlier churches—the previous St. Peter Basilica was replaced with the current one and fire destroyed St. Paul Basilica—has been observed in Rome since the eleventh century. In the universal liturgical calendar, this is an optional memorial; if one chooses to observe it, it has proper readings that must be used.

Optional Memorial of the Dedication of the Basilica of Sts. Peter and Paul, Apostles

Today's gospel passage follows the Matthean narrative of John the Baptist's death and Jesus' feeding of five thousand men using five loaves and two fish. After the meal is finished, Jesus instructs his disciple to get into a boat and cross an unnamed body of water while he goes to an unnamed mountain to pray. While the boat is being tossed about by waves on the sea, Jesus walks on the water toward his disciples in it. This much of the narrative comes from Mark's Gospel (6:45–52), which is one of the sources the author of Matthew's Gospel used for his work.

Unique Matthean material is now added. Peter, attempting to establish Jesus' identity, says, "Lord, if it is you, command me to come to you on the water" (14:28). Jesus obliges, and Peter walks on water, until he becomes afraid and begins to sink. In this unique Matthean Petrine material, the author attempts to establish Peter as a leader in the church. Other uniquely Petrine stories in Matthew portray Peter as a rock and one who is sent into the whole world to make disciples.

The Matthean Jesus tells his disciples and Peter not to be afraid. Fear is the opposite of faith. Many people think that the opposite of faith is doubt, but that is erroneous. Doubt is good because it makes us plumb more deeply what we initially believe. Fear inhibits trust. As long as Peter trusts Jesus, he walks on water with him. It is only when Peter notices the wind that he becomes frightened; then he begins to sink and needs Jesus to grab his hand and pull into the boat. That's why Jesus addresses Peter, saying, "You of little faith . . ." (14:31).

In celebrating the Memorial of the Dedication of the Basilica of Sts. Peter and Paul, Apostles, we, the church take time to recognize how our fear gets in the way of our trust. The Matthean Jesus wants us to trust God like the birds of the sky; they do not store food, yet God takes care of them. He wants us to trust God like the flowers that grow and blossom in the field; they do not make clothes, yet God takes care of them. Our trust in God should be like Jesus on the cross; he entrusted his life to his Father, who raised him from the dead. As members of the Church, our little faith, like Peter's, is enough to trust God and grow stronger every time we trust again.

Meditation: In what specific ways do you trust God?

Prayer: Almighty Father, you never cease to care for everyone and everything you have created. Strengthen our little faith, that we may take up our cross and follow you. Fill us, your church, with the guidance of the

Holy Spirit. We ask this through our Lord Jesus Christ, your Son, who lives and reigns with you and the Holy Spirit, one God, forever and ever. Amen.

✤ November 30
Feast of St. Andrew, Apostle

Believe and Proclaim

Romans 10:9–18

Scripture: ". . . [I]f you confess with your lips that Jesus is Lord and believe in your heart that God raised him from the dead, you will be saved" (Rom 10:9).

Reflection: The pericope from Paul's letter to the Romans assigned for this Feast of St. Andrew begins in the middle of a sentence. Paul has just presented his argument about how God will save both Jews and Gentiles. Since the Gentiles have accepted God's offer of salvation and the Jews have rejected it, Paul writes that his prayer for the Jews "is that they may be saved" (10:1). He adds, "I can testify that they have a zeal for God, but it is not enlightened" (10:2). They think that they can earn righteousness, that is a healthy relationship with God, and fail to understand that God's righteousness is a gift offered to all believers through Christ Jesus. Paul declares that righteousness comes from faith. Therefore, if one confesses with one's lips that Jesus is Lord and believes in one's heart that God raised him from the dead, that person will be saved.

In Pauline thought, belief leads to justification. "[O]ne believes with the heart and so is justified," writes Paul, "and one confesses with the mouth and so is saved" (10:10). Since "Christ is the end of the law so that there may be righteousness for everyone who believes" (10:4), there is "no distinction between Jew and Greek; the same Lord is Lord of all and is generous to all who call on him" (10:12). In other words, all people are offered the gift of God's justification through faith in Christ. Once God chose a people—Hebrews, Israelites, Jews—but now God has chosen all people—Jews and Gentiles.

This passage is chosen for the Feast of St. Andrew, an apostle, because the word "apostle" means "sent" and that is the next part of Paul's argument. He asks a series of rhetorical questions to make his point: "... [H]ow are [people] to call on one in whom they have not believed? And how are they to believe in one of whom they have never heard? And how are they to hear without someone to proclaim him? And how are they to proclaim him unless they are sent?" (10:14–15) Thus, faith is the result of hearing the proclamation of the gospel that Jesus died and God raised Christ from the dead, and this proclamation comes through the word of Christ.

Andrew, brother of Peter, was sent by Jesus with the basic proclamation of the Pauline gospel: Jesus died and God raised Christ from the dead. Paul's broad vision oozes with God's love and care for all people—Jews and Gentiles. Paul envisions that all people will ultimately be incorporated into Christ through the proclamation of the gospel and by calling upon a generous Lord. Needless to say, Paul's vision remains to be realized. We, like Andrew, have heard the proclamation of the gospel, and we have believed it. And now we are sent to proclaim it to others, who will, hopefully, hear it, believe it, and proclaim it in turn.

Meditation: To whom have you been sent with the gospel?

Prayer: Ever-living God, you gave your Son, Jesus, apostles and sent them into the world to proclaim the good news of what you had done in him. Fill us with the same Spirit that you bestowed upon St. Andrew, that what we hear with our ears we may confess with our lips: Jesus is Lord to your glory, Father, forever and ever. Amen.

Manly

Matthew 4:18–22

Scripture: "As [Jesus] walked by the sea of Galilee, he saw two brothers, Simon, who is called Peter, and Andrew his brother, casting a net into the sea—for they were fishermen. And he said to them, 'Follow me, and I will

Feast of St. Andrew, Apostle

make you fish for people.' Immediately they left their nets and followed him" (Matt 4:18–20).

Reflection: In Matthew's Gospel, the first disciples are called after Jesus' threefold temptation, which is followed by a quote from the prophet Isaiah explaining why Jesus went to Galilee and Jesus' preaching that the kingdom of heaven is at hand. The first two men called to be Jesus' disciples are Simon and Andrew. They are fishing in the Sea of Galilee. All Jesus has to say is, "Follow me, and I will make you fish for people" (4:19), and they leave their nets and follow him.

Matthew's narrative is taken almost word for word from Mark's Gospel (1:16–17), one of the author's sources for his own work. The passage is proclaimed on the Feast of St. Andrew, the apostle, because it mentions him by name and identifies him as Simon's brother. In John's Gospel, it is Andrew who is first called by Jesus; Andrew, in turn, finds Simon and brings him to Jesus.

Worthy of our reflection on this Feast of St. Andrew is Jesus' invitation: "Follow me, and I will make you fish for people" (4:19). To follow another implies that a person comes after; in this case Andrew accepts Jesus' authority and pursues him. Following also implies imitation; those who follow Jesus imitate his lifestyle, his preaching, his teaching. In time, a follower takes the place of his master, as did Andrew, one of the Twelve, along with all the responsibility that accompanies the position.

Those who follow Jesus are made fishers of people. This means that they catch others; others witness the lifestyle of followers and this awakens in them a desire to follow Jesus, too. Being caught implies dying; a caught fish is usually a dead fish. We die to one way of life in order to embrace another way of life. Also, there is a hint here of Jesus' own death and resurrection. And, since according to tradition, Andrew died on an X-shaped cross, the passage refers to the apostle whom Jesus caught with a simple invitation to follow him.

In our own day and time, Jesus' invitation is still issued to any who will hear it. Through us, God calls others to follow his Son, to live a life that both inwardly and outwardly manifests the values of Jesus. Our words, our deeds, our very identity either catches people or leaves them befuddled. Andrew's name means "manly"; Andrew was a strong follower of Jesus, becoming a fisher of people. As such, he is a worthy model of discipleship.

Mediation: In what specific ways do you catch others for Christ? In what specific ways have others caught you for Jesus?

Prayer: Ever-living God, your Son invited Andrew to follow him in proclaiming the arrival of your kingdom, and the brother of Simon responded wholeheartedly. Help us to hear Jesus' invitation every day, and fill us with the Holy Spirit that our words and deeds may catch more followers for our Lord Jesus Christ, who lives and reigns with you and the Holy Spirit. You are one God, forever and ever. Amen.

✤ December 8
Solemnity of the Immaculate Conception of the Blessed Virgin Mary

Idolatry

Genesis 3:9–15, 20

Scripture: "The LORD God said to the serpent, . . . 'I will put enmity between you and the woman, and between your offspring and hers; he will strike your head, and you will strike his heel'" (Gen 3:14–15).

Reflection: Even though December 8, the Solemnity of the Immaculate Conception of the Blessed Virgin Mary, may fall on a Sunday, the celebration of the feast is transferred to the Saturday before or the Monday after (without the transference of the holy day obligation) because the Sundays of Advent take precedent over this day. The first pericope from the Book of Genesis is a small part of a much larger story about the serpent in the garden. It is important to state that the serpent is not the devil or Satan; all the author of Genesis states is that "the serpent was more crafty than any other wild animal that the LORD God had made" (3:1).

After the man and woman have eaten "of the fruit of the tree that is in the middle of the garden" (3:3), the LORD God comes "walking in the garden at the time of the evening breeze" (3:8), but "the man and his wife hid themselves from the presence of the LORD God among the trees of the garden" (3:9). After the Creator calls to the couple, "Where are you?" (3:9)—an interesting question for the all-knowing Deity!—the man answers, "I heard the sound of you in the garden, and I was afraid, because I was naked; and I hid myself" (3:10). In turn, God asks two questions: "Who told you that you were naked? Have you eaten from the tree of which I commanded you not to eat?" (3:11)

The dialogue about nakedness is a metaphor for shame. Jewish culture was one of honor and shame. Basically, a man could only be honored, and a woman could only be shamed. It is important to notice that in this pre-exilic account that the man becomes an object of shame, and his first attempt at giving an explanation to the LORD God is to shift the shame to the woman. "The woman whom you gave to be with me, she gave me fruit from the tree, and I ate" (3:12), states the man to the LORD God. Next, the woman shifts the shame to the serpent, telling the LORD God, "The serpent tricked me, and I ate" (3:13).

Nakedness or shame has never been an issue in the narrative until the couple self-incriminate themselves. The LORD God, as indicated above, is not portrayed as omniscient, since he has to investigate the breaking of the commandment not to eat of the tree in the middle of the garden by asking a series of questions and tracing the blame from the man to the woman to the serpent. Once the LORD God has gotten to the culprit, he curses them in reverse order.

A curse does not mean the contemporary cultural practice of using vulgar language. A biblical curse is an invocation of misfortune upon a person. The crafty serpent will crawl upon its belly and eat dust all the days of its life. The woman will have greater pangs in childbearing, and the man will have to work hard, tilling the soil and digging out thorns and thistles, to feed his family. These curses, omitted from today's pericope, are mythological, that is, they explain why things are the way they are. They answer the questions: Why does a snake crawl on the ground? Why is giving birth painful? Why is agriculture laborious? And, though it is not a part of today's pericope, it answers this question: Why do people die? The answer is simple: The LORD God curses them, declaring, "By the sweat of your face you shall eat bread until you return to the ground, for out of it you were taken; you are dust, and to dust you shall return" (3:19).

The reason this pericope is chosen as the first reading for the Solemnity of the Immaculate Conception of the Blessed Virgin Mary is found in verse 15: The LORD God says to the serpent, "I will put enmity between you and the woman, and between your offspring and hers; he will strike your head, and you will strike his heel." This verse is known as the protoevangelium or the pre-gospel. This is the first announcement of salvation from the first or original sin. Statues of Our Lady of Grace present the Blessed Virgin Mary standing on the earth with her foot on the head of a serpent. She was immaculately conceived, that is, she "was redeemed from the moment of her

Solemnity of the Immaculate Conception of the Blessed Virgin Mary

conception," states the *Catechism of the Catholic Church* (491). By a special grace and privilege of God and by virtue of the merits of the Son she was to bear, she was "preserved immune from all stain of original sin" (491).

While it is not obvious to modern readers, the intended readers of the Book of Genesis knew that the serpent was a sign of the pagan god Baal. Idolatry was a major problem for God's people throughout their history; it is reflected in this story. Idolatry is a major problem today, although the term is not used. People worship creatures rather than the Creator. Homes, cars, boats take much care while the homeless die of starvation. Pets are often treated better than people who are aborted or euthanized. Back yard storage sheds overflow with stuff, while others have nothing. While looking at this type of idolatry does not require us to recognize that we are naked, it should at the minimum make us ashamed.

The Blessed Virgin Mary escaped such idolatry. By conceiving and giving birth to our Savior, Jesus Christ, she showed the world how to cooperate with God's grace and strike the head of the crafty serpent.

Meditation: What is your idolatry? In what way can God's grace help you to remove it?

Prayer: Father of our Lord Jesus Christ, you prepared the world for the birth of your Son by preserving Mary of Nazareth from original sin through the power of the Holy Spirit. Remove all idolatry from us that we may respond to your grace and your offer of salvation through the same Jesus Christ, who is Lord forever and ever. Amen.

Adoption

Ephesians 1:3–6, 11–12

Scripture: "Blessed be the God and Father of our Lord Jesus Christ, who has blessed us in Christ with every spiritual blessing in the heavenly places, just as he chose us in Christ before the foundation of the world to be holy and blameless before him in love" (Eph 1:3).

Reflection: Part of the opening of the post-Pauline reflection, known as Paul's Letter to the Ephesians, is chosen as the second reading for the Solemnity of the Immaculate Conception of the Blessed Virgin Mary, a feast that is never celebrated on a Sunday. The passage begins with a beatitude, a declaration that God is blessed and that God has blessed the reader, the believer, on earth, with every spiritual blessing that could possible come from heaven.

The beatitude gives way to the concept of predestination. Predestination does not mean that some people are predestined for heaven and some for hell. In this post-Pauline use, it refers to God's omniscient plan to choose all people to be his people and "to be holy and blameless before him in love" (3:4) before he created the world. In other words, God has always desired that all people be like him—holy—and blameless—without shame (sin)—living the life of the Trinity in love. Once people brought sin into God's holy creation, he destined them "for adoption as his children" (1:5) through the salvation accomplished by Christ Jesus' death and resurrection. This he did "according to the good pleasure of his will, to the praise of his glorious grace that he freely bestowed on" all through Christ (1:5–6). In other words, God took great pleasure in gracing people so that they could cooperate with him in their salvation.

The pericope omits verses 7–10 in which the post-Pauline author writes about the redemption from sin that was accomplished by Christ's blood, and how this was nothing but grace. God's wisdom, insight, and will have now been revealed in Christ "as a plan for the fullness of time, to gather up all things in him, things in heaven and things on earth" (1:10). This means that all people "have also obtained an inheritance, having been destined according to the purpose of [God] who accomplishes all things according to his counsel and will" (1:11). While all await the final gathering into Christ, those have received this hope first "live for the praise of [God's] glory" (1:12).

The human being who best illustrates the post-Pauline author's words is Mary of Nazareth. She was chosen before the world was created to be the mother of Christ Jesus. She was destined, preserved from sin from the moment of her conception. Mary was saved before her Son brought redemption through his passion, death, and resurrection. She was given an inheritance before the inheritance was revealed. The Virgin of Nazareth was God's instrument for accomplishing his will to save his creation to the praise of his glory.

Solemnity of the Immaculate Conception of the Blessed Virgin Mary

"God, infinitely perfect and blessed in himself, in a plan of sheer goodness freely created man [and woman] to make [them] share in his own blessed life," states the *Catechism of the Catholic Church* (1). God calls people "to seek him, to know him, to love him with all his strength" (1). The one person who did this to the full was the Blessed Virgin Mary. With her all we can do is praise God for what he has done and continues to do for us.

Meditation: In what ways do you know, love, and serve God?

Prayer: All-knowing Father, after freely creating people who sinned, you continued to share your divine life with them. In the fullness of time you prepared the Blessed Virgin Mary to be the mother of your Son that we might know you, love you, and serve you in this world and be happy with you forever. Through the inspiration of the Holy Spirit, guide our footsteps to you. We ask this through our Lord Jesus Christ, your Son, who lives and reigns with you and the Holy Spirit, one God, forever and ever. Amen.

Graced

Luke 1:26–38

Scripture: The angel Gabriel came to Mary and said, "Greetings, favored one! The Lord is with you" (Luke 1:28).

Reflection: Although we hear this gospel, known as the annunciation, many times during the liturgical year, especially on memorials and feasts of the Blessed Virgin Mary during Advent and Christmas, it is important to hear it again on the Solemnity of the Immaculate Conception of the Blessed Virgin Mary because it portrays her as God's favored one, God's graced one, with whom is the Most High. ". . . [I]n order for Mary to be able to give the free assent of her faith to the announcement of her vocation," states the *Catechism of the Catholic Church*, "it was necessary that she be wholly borne by God's grace" (490). The dogma of the Immaculate Conception was defined by Pope Pius IX in 1854. He declared, "The most Blessed Virgin Mary was, from the first moment of her conception, by a singular grace and privilege of almighty God and by virtue of the merits of Jesus Christ, Savior of the human race, preserved immune from all stain of original sin" (491). The *Catechism* adds, "The Father blessed Mary more than any other created person..." (492).

Luke's Gospel, written around 90 AD, presents the annunciation of Gabriel to Mary of the birth of Jesus as a parallel to the annunciation of Gabriel to Zechariah of the birth of John the Baptist. These parallel accounts also illustrate a Lukan literary technique, namely, a story about a man is usually followed by a story about a woman.

Luke's account oozes grace, God's own divine life. Gabriel, whose name means "God's strength," greets the Virgin of Nazareth as the favored or graced one, the one with whom is the Lord. Gabriel explains to Mary that "the Holy Spirit will come upon [her], and the power of the Most High will overshadow [her]; therefore the child to be born will be holy; he will be called Son of God" (1:35). Mary is wrapped in grace; she is flooded with grace; she is baptized in grace. Like the cloud that overshadowed and protected the people of Israel from all harm, Mary is overshadowed and protected by God's very life. Grace enables her to agree to do God's will, to be "the servant of the Lord" (1:38).

The grace bestowed upon Mary through her immaculate conception and annunciation is offered to us on the day of baptism and again on the day of confirmation. God offers us a share in the salvation accomplished by the death and resurrection of Mary's Son. Once we say yes, we become cooperators with God and desire to do his will. His purpose probably will be revealed to us gradually, in stages, as we are able to understand it. It requires discernment on our part, and that discernment can be had only through prayer and reflection on the events of our lives in conjunction with such biblical passages as this one. This is a process that lasts a lifetime; there is never a time when we can declare that we are finished. At every step, we can join Mary in declaring, "Here am I, the servant of the Lord; let it be with me according to [the] word" (1:38).

Meditation: What have been the stages of your cooperation with God in order to do his will? What grace was bestowed on you at each stage?

Prayer: Most High God, you surrounded the Blessed Virgin Mary with your own divine life in order to enable her to do your will and conceive and give birth to your Son. Grace us with the Holy Spirit that we may know your will and do it with enthusiasm. We ask this through our Lord Jesus

Solemnity of the Immaculate Conception of the Blessed Virgin Mary

Christ, who lives and reigns with you, Father, and the Holy Spirit, one God, forever and ever. Amen.

✤ December 12
Feast of Our Lady of Guadalupe

Silence

(1) Zechariah 2:14–17 (2:10–13)

Scripture: "Sing and rejoice, O daughter Zion! For lo, I [, the LORD of hosts,] will come and dwell in your midst, says the LORD. Many nations shall join themselves to the LORD on that day, and shall be my people, and I will dwell in your midst" (Zech 2:14–15 [2:10–11]).

Reflection: Four days after marking the Solemnity of the Immaculate Conception of the Blessed Virgin Mary, the church celebrates a feast in her honor as Our Lady of Guadalupe. The first option for a first reading for this feast is a very short pericope from the prophet Zechariah. It is a part of a short speech addressed to the Jews in Babylonian exile. It urges them to return to "Daughter Zion" (2:14/2:10), that is, Jerusalem, which the LORD of hosts promises to restore and in which to establish his dwelling place.

This passage is presented as the first option for the first reading on the Feast of Our Lady of Guadalupe, who appeared on the slopes of the Hill of Tepeyac outside of Mexico City, Mexico, to Juan Diego on December 9, 1531, as a fifteen- or sixteen-year-old girl surrounded by light, because Mary's womb is considered to be a new Jerusalem in which the Son of God has come to dwell in our midst. After reporting his vision, Diego asked the lady for a sign to prove her identity as the Blessed Virgin Mary. She told him to gather Castilian roses from the top of Tepeyac Hill and carry them in his peasant tilma (cloak). When he opened the cloak on December 12, 1531, the roses fell to the floor, and in their place was the image of the Virgin of Guadalupe, miraculously imprinted on the fabric.

Feast of Our Lady of Guadalupe

The image of Our Lady of Guadalupe presents a four-petal flower on her womb indicating life and movement. Furthermore, the sash tied around her waist is a sign of pregnancy, even as part of her dress bulges to indicate that she is with child. Thus is fulfilled the words of Zechariah that the LORD "has roused himself from his holy dwelling" (2:17/2:13) in heaven and come to dwell in our midst. The proper disposition of those who understand all this is silence. Zechariah states, "Be silent, all people, before the LORD" (2:17/2:13).

While silence may be a thing of the past in a world dominated by the noise produced from all types of electronic devices and vehicles and machines, it is a proper response to this feast. We take God for granted. We get so caught up in ourselves—even in a church—that we fail to recognize the LORD who dwells there. In a day when even our churches often become places where people hold conversations, the Feast of Our Lady of Guadalupe gives us permission to put our finger up to our lips and to say, "Shh-hhh!" We need to be able to appreciate the presence of the LORD of hosts.

Meditation: What role does silence play in your prayer?

Prayer: We sing and rejoice in your presence, LORD of hosts. We praise you for revealing Our Lady of Guadalupe to the nations. As we celebrate this day in her honor, grant us silence in our hearts that we may recognize your Trinitarian life within us. You are one God—Father, Son, and Holy Spirit—forever and ever. Amen.

Signs

(2) Revelation 11:19a, 12:1–6a, 10ab

Scripture: "A great portent appeared in heaven: a woman clothed with the sun, with the moon under her feet, and on her head a crown of twelve stars" (Rev 12:1).

Reflection: The second option for the first reading on the Feast of Our Lady of Guadalupe is pieced together from parts of seven verses from the Book of Revelation. The narrator writes that "God's temple in heaven was opened, and the ark of his covenant was seen within his temple" (19a). While the usual signs of the divine presence are omitted in the second part of the verse—namely, lightning, rumblings, peals of thunder, earthquake, hail—the reader knows that the ark of the covenant was the box that contained the tablets of the Law given to Moses by God, a jar of manna from the dessert, and Aaron's staff used to part the Sea of Reeds after the Hebrews escape from Egypt. This verse about the ark of the covenant introduces the pericope because Mary is a new ark; her womb is like the box that "contained" God's presence.

John of Patmos, the given author of the book, peers into the divine realm before narrating what is happening astrologically. A sign or portent is given. A woman appears "clothed with the sun, with the moon under her feet, and on her head a crown of twelve stars" (12:1). The portent is very much like Joseph's dream in the Book of Genesis of "the sun, the moon, and eleven stars... bowing down to [him]" (37:9)—representing his father, mother, and eleven brothers.

This passage is chosen for the Feast of Our Lady of Guadalupe because her image depicts her in just this manner. The sun shines behind her; she rests her feet on the moon; and stars surround her. Furthermore, like the portent in Revelation, she is pregnant, signified by the sash at her waist. She gives birth "to a son, a male child, who is to rule all the nations with a rod of iron" (12:5). He brings God's salvation and the kingdom of God and the authority of his Messiah.

The Book of Revelation presents another sign or portent: "a great red dragon, with seven heads and ten horns, and seven diadems on his heads" (12:3). At the time the Book of Revelation was written late in the first century AD, Christians thought of the seven Roman emperors with their seven crowns and the ten Seleucid rulers of Palestine before them as the corporate enemy of God which tried to wipe out the child born of the woman destined to rule all the nations. But God was ready to protect both the child and his mother even after the dragon was hurled down to the earth by Michael. The salvation accomplished in heaven will also be accomplished on the earth through the Messiah.

The passage from Revelation overflows with signs of God's presence. The appearance of Our Lady of Guadalupe to Juan Diego on December 9, 1531, and the image she left on his tilma (cloak) on December 12, 1531, are more signs of the divine presence. Our daily lives are filled with God's presence if we stop long enough to notice them and appreciate their beauty.

Feast of Our Lady of Guadalupe

Daily, we can witness the sunrise and sunset. Monthly, a full moon rise can dazzle us. The gentle rain after a drought can make us aware of God's grace. The smallest things—tiny plants from lettuce and radish seeds in the garden—can serve as signs of God's presence just as well as an appearance of the Blessed Virgin Mary or a portent in the sky.

Meditation: What recent sign has awakened you to God's presence?

Prayer: Almighty God, all of your creation manifests your presence to your people. Make us aware of all of your blessings, especially that of Our Lady of Guadalupe and the child she bore, our Lord Jesus Christ, who lives and reigns with you and the Holy Spirit, one God, forever and ever. Amen.

Fear

(1) Luke 1:26-38

Scripture: "The angel [Gabriel] said to [Mary], 'Do not be afraid, Mary, for you have found favor with God. And now you will conceive in your womb and bear a son, and you will name him Jesus'" (Luke 1:30–31).

Reflection: The first response most people make to something new is fear. Ask someone, "How about going on a hike in the woods?" and get the response, "I fear there may be snakes." Ask, "Have you tried anything off the new menu at your favorite restaurant?" and you will get, "No, the new menu does not have anything that will taste good." Ask, "Would you be willing to serve as a reader at Mass?" and you will get, "I fear I will make a mistake."

Fear keeps us away from life. And we are not talking about a healthy fear, like fearing sunstroke on a 95-degree summer day, or fearing an auto accident because one cannot see well at night, or fear of getting into a small boat on a lake without a life jacket when a person cannot swim. Those types of fear keep us safe. However, some kinds of fear keep us from living and growing. Change brings life; fear often brings death.

God seems always to be about change and the elimination of fear. When the angel Gabriel (whose name means "God's strength") visits "a virgin engaged to a man whose names was Joseph" (1:27) in "a town in Galilee called Nazareth" (1:26), one of the first things he tells her is: "Do not be afraid, Mary, for you have found favor with God" (1:30). Once he quiets her fear and opens her to the possibility of change, she is ready to accept all the newness that God offers. This newness takes several forms: A virgin will conceive a child by the Holy Spirit; a virgin will give birth to the Son of the Most High. Gabriel gives Mary a sign to verify all this newness: Her relative "Elizabeth in her old age has also conceived a son; and this is the sixth month for her who was said to be barren" (1:36). In the next scene in Luke's Gospel (the second option for today's gospel), Mary visits Elizabeth to see this sign.

Likewise, Juan Diego needed a sign that the Blessed Virgin Mary appeared to him on Tepeyac Hill. No one wanted to believe the new story that the Mother of God had appeared in Mexico. So, Mary imprinted herself on Diego's tilma (cloak) after he gathered roses which were not in season. The Basilica of Our Lady of Guadalupe was built and became the most visited Marian shrine in the world. This newness of faith continues to spread from Mexico City throughout the world.

What was true of Mary and Juan Diego is also true for all who fear change. God seems to be at the forefront of change. In other words, growth in holiness (wholeness) in relationship with God is required through Sunday and Holy Day Mass, through fasting and abstaining on appointed days, through the confession of sins and reception of Holy Communion, through sacrificial giving to support the work of the church. Commonly known as the precepts of the Catholic Church, these rules insure the minimum of growth in those who have said yes to God's will, like Mary of Nazareth, like Juan Diego.

Meditation: What fear gets in your way of growth in your relationship with God? How can you overcome that fear in order to change and experience new life?

Prayer: Most High God, you overshadowed Mary of Nazareth with the Holy Spirit so that she could conceive and give birth to your only-begotten Son, Jesus Christ. As we celebrate the Feast of Our Lady of Guadalupe, open our minds and hearts to your will, that we may grow in your grace and experience the new life Christ won for us. We ask this through the same Christ our Lord, who lives and reigns with you and the Holy Spirit, one God, forever and ever. Amen.

Visitation

(2) Luke 1:39–47

Scripture: "In those days Mary set out and went with haste to a Judean town in the hill country, where she entered the house of Zechariah and greeted Elizabeth" (Luke 1:39–40).

Reflection: The second option for a gospel reading for the Feast of Our Lady of Guadalupe is the passage from Luke's Gospel that is commonly called the visitation. This uniquely Lukan pericope brings together the two unique Lukan annunciation stories, namely, Gabriel's annunciation to Zechariah about the birth of John the Baptist and Gabriel's annunciation to Mary about the birth of Jesus. Gabriel made Zechariah dumb as a sign of John's impending birth, and Gabriel gave Mary the sign of Elizabeth's six-month pregnancy. With Mary's visit to Elizabeth the two accounts—one announcement to a man and one to a woman, another unique Lukan feature—are brought together.

"Elizabeth was filled with the Holy Spirit" (1:41), just like Mary had "the Holy Spirit . . . come upon her" (1:35). This meeting of Holy Spirit and Holy Spirit causes John the Baptist to leap for joy in Elizabeth's womb, and prepares for his role as precursor of the Messiah. Elizabeth's first beatitude—"Blessed are you [, Mary,] among women, and blessed is the fruit of your womb" (1:42)—echoes Gabriel's greeting to Mary: "Greetings, favored one! The Lord is with you" (1:28). The foci are the two pregnancies. The image of Our Lady of Guadalupe depicts Mary with a sash around her waist, indicating that she is pregnant.

Elizabeth's second beatitude—". . . Blessed is she who believed that there would be a fulfillment of what was spoken to her by the Lord" (1:45)—echoes Mary's response to Gabriel: "Here am I, the servant of the Lord; let it be with me according to your word" (1:38). Another unique Lukan feature is the hymn, modeled on Hannah's song in 1 Samuel 2:1–10, that Mary sings in response to Elizabeth's second beatitude. The gospel provides only the first verse of this song that summarizes the rest of Luke's Gospel.

As social creatures, human beings do a lot of visiting with friends from high school and college, with relatives, such as parents, in-laws, brothers and sisters, uncles and aunts, after church over coffee and doughnuts, while enjoying a pot-luck dinner. While we are not conscious that we, like Mary, carry Christ with us to others, a meal prayer, a caution about a prejudice, or the putting to rest of a rumor may be all that is needed to awaken another to the presence of Christ. Mary, both in Luke's Gospel and in her appearance as Our Lady of Guadalupe, points toward her Son, who brings salvation to the whole world.

Meditation: In what recent visit with another did you become aware of Christ's presence?

Prayer: Almighty God, to the people of Mexico you revealed Mary as Our Lady of Guadalupe. Through the intercession of the Mother of God, help us bring Christ's gospel to all we meet. May we always magnify you, Father, through our Lord Jesus Christ, your Son, in the unity of the Holy Spirit, forever and ever. Amen.

✠ December 26
Feast of St. Stephen, First Martyr

Like Jesus

Acts 6:8–10, 7:54–59

Scripture: "While [the people] were stoning Stephen, he prayed, 'Lord Jesus, receive my spirit.' Then he knelt down and cried out in a loud voice, 'Lord, do not hold this sin against them.' When he had said this, he died" (Acts 7:59–60).

Reflection: The day after the Solemnity of the Nativity of the Lord (Christmas), the church celebrates the martyrdom of St. Stephen, that is, his nativity into eternal life. Stephen, who is considered to be the first Christian martyr, is the subject of two long chapters in the Acts of the Apostles, the second volume of Luke's two-volume work—the first volume is Luke's Gospel. Today's first reading is a very short pericope from the longer narrative at 6:1—8:1.

Luke models Stephen in the Acts on Jesus in the gospel. In other words, Stephen is an image of Christ. Just as Jesus is repeatedly indicated to be full of the Holy Spirit (3:22, 4:1, 14) in Luke's Gospel, Stephen is full of the Holy Spirit in the Acts (6:3, 5, 10, 7:55). In Luke's Gospel, Jesus cast out demons, healed a number of people, and cleansed lepers; in the Acts, Stephen "did great wonders and signs among the people" (6:8). Jesus, known for his wisdom, delivers his inaugural discourse (Luke 4:14–32); likewise, people "could not withstand the wisdom and the spirit with which [Stephen] spoke" (Acts 6:10), especially as he gives his discourse, a summary of the Hebrew Bible (Old Testament) (Acts 7:2–53).

In Luke's Gospel, Jesus is accused by false witnesses (20:19–20, 22:66–67; 23:2, 5), as in the Acts is Stephen "set up [with] false witnesses" (6:13) by the synagogue of the Freedmen. After Jesus is baptized, the heaven was opened (Luke 4:21); before he dies, Stephen gazes "into heaven and [sees] the glory of God and Jesus standing at the right hand of God" (Acts 7:55). Jesus is crucified outside of Jerusalem; Stephen is dragged out of the city and stoned (Acts 7:58–59).

Because Luke characterizes Jesus as a pray-er throughout the gospel, he prays twice before he dies on the cross. "Father, into your hands I commend my spirit" (Luke 23:46), he says. Likewise, before he dies Stephen prays, "Lord Jesus, receive my spirit" (Acts 7:59). And just as Jesus asks his Father to forgive those who have crucified him "for they do not know what they are doing" (Luke 23:34), so does Stephen pray for those who are stoning him, "Lord, do not hold this sin against them" (Acts 7:59).

Luke's point in painting the picture of Stephen to look like Jesus is to emphasize that if we want to receive our crown, we must be shaped into the image of Christ, like Stephen was. We need to be filled with God's Holy Spirit so that the Holy One can fill our mouths with his wisdom and accomplish great deeds through our hands. We may not be liked; we may have rumors started about us; we may even be persecuted, but prayer enables us to forgiven our enemies and to entrust ourselves into God's hands. Stephen is a model of how to live a Christian life. The opposite model is made up of those who are stiff-necked, "uncircumcised in heart and ears, [who] are forever opposing the Holy Spirit" (Acts 7:51).

Meditation: In what specific ways do you imitate Stephen (Jesus)?

Prayer: Heaven is your throne, almighty God, and the earth is your footstool. Through the intercession of St. Stephen, grant us the wisdom of the Holy Spirit that we may speak your words and do your deeds to the glory of your name. We ask this through our Lord Jesus Christ, your Son, who lives and reigns with you and the Holy Spirit, one God, forever and ever. Amen.

Fulfilled Words

Matthew 10:17–22

Feast of St. Stephen, First Martyr

Scripture: Jesus said to his twelve disciples, "Beware of [wolves], for they will hand you over to councils and flog you in their synagogues; and you will be dragged before governors and kings because of me, as a testimony to them and the Gentiles" (Matt 10:17–18).

Reflection: The six verses that form today's gospel passage are taken from the second of five major discourses that Jesus gives in Matthew's Gospel. The second sermon is known as the missionary discourse (10:1–11:1). Because the author of Matthew's Gospel understands Jesus to be a new Moses, who wrote the five books of the Torah (Genesis, Exodus, Leviticus, Numbers, Deuteronomy), Jesus gives five major speeches, discourses, or sermons. Today's pericope consists of missionary warnings; it is chosen as the gospel for the Feast of St. Stephen because Matthew's words are seen as fulfilled in Stephen's missionary work in the Acts of the Apostles (6:1–8:1).

Jesus warns his disciples that they will be handed over to councils, as Stephen was (Acts 6:12). Jesus tells his disciples not to worry about what they are to speak or what they are to say, for what they are to stay will be given to them "by the Spirit of [their] Father speaking through [them]" (10:20), as Stephen speaks with "the wisdom and the Spirit" (Acts 6:10). Jesus tells his disciples that family members will betray each other "to death" (10:21), as Stephen is betrayed (Acts 6:13) to death (Acts 7:58–60). Jesus tells his disciples that the "one who endures to the end will be saved" (10:22), as Stephen is saved (Acts 7:56). Thus, the Matthean Jesus' discourse to missionaries is fulfilled in Stephen, a missioner.

The missionary activity of the church continues today. The *Catechism of the Catholic Church* states, ". . . [T]he Church's mission is not an addition to that of Christ and the Holy Spirit, but is its sacrament: in her whole being and in all her members, the Church is sent to announce, bear witness, make present, and spread the mystery of the communion of the Holy Trinity" (738).

Throughout the world, missionaries bring the gospel to those who have not yet heard it. Sometimes they are handed over. Sometimes they are betrayed to death. "The Spirit prepares men [and women] and goes out to them with his grace, in order to draw them to Christ. The Spirit manifests the risen Lord to them, recalls his word to them, and opens their minds to the understanding of his Death and Resurrection. He makes present the mystery of Christ, supremely in the Eucharist, in order to reconcile them, to bring them into communion with God, that they may 'bear much fruit,'" states the *Catechism* (737). Thus, as Stephen fulfilled Jesus' words in the Acts of the Apostles, so we, hopefully, continue to fulfill them today.

Meditation: What words of Jesus have you fulfilled in your life as a missionary?

Prayer: God of St. Stephen, you promise to fill your missionaries with the Holy Spirit that they can announce the death and resurrection of your Son. Remove all worry from our minds and pour out on us the same Holy Spirit that we may bring the gospel wherever we go. We ask this through our Lord Jesus Christ, who lives and reigns with you, Father, and the Holy Spirit, one God, forever and ever. Amen.

✠ December 27
Feast of St. John, Apostle and Evangelist

Fellowship

1 John 1:1-4

Scripture: "We declare to you what was from the beginning, what we have heard, what we have seen with our eyes, what we have looked at and touched with our hands, concerning the word of life . . ." (1 John 1:1).

Reflection: On the second day after Christmas, the church celebrates the Feast of St. John, apostle and evangelist. The first reading is the prologue to the first letter of John which echoes themes found in the prologue to John's Gospel (1:1-18). Written near the end of the first century AD, 1 John is more like a tract or a homily than a letter. The author, coming out of the same Johannine school as the authors of John's Gospel, attempts to apply the Christian message to the situation of his readers. The prologue is focused on the humanity of Jesus.

The "word of life" (1:1) refers both to the person of Jesus and his message. Jesus was the "word of life" spoken by God and made flesh. He revealed "the eternal life that was with the Father" (1:2) through his teaching. What the author declares "was from the beginning" (1:1) has now been heard, seen, looked at, and touched, that is, the person of Jesus Christ.

The purpose of the word becoming flesh and revealing eternal life is fellowship from two points of view. First, fellowship exists among believers, who form a community of members knit together by their faith. Second, the fellowship of the community also exists "with the Father and with his Son Jesus Christ" (1:3). Through the incarnation, the death, and the resurrection of the Son, heaven and earth have been united in one faith.

The author expresses the fact that he is preparing this document self-consciously by writing, "We are writing these things so that our joy may be complete" (1:4), that is, so that the testimony of the witnesses may guarantee the truth of the letter as it is shared with others and draws them into fellowship.

In a fellowship that exists between believers and between believers and God, who is in himself a fellowship of Father, Son, and Holy Spirit, the community is placed ahead of the individual. In a culture that thrives on individualism, this becomes a difficult concept to grasp. In the four verses of the prologue, the author never uses the pronoun "I"; he uses "we" eight times, "us" two times, and "our" four times. He desires to share the common interest in eternal life with others so that the joy of their human companionship can be complete with the joy of their divine companionship.

An extreme individualism subverts fellowship. "All that matters is what I think," many people say. "What's in it for me?" asks another. "You have to look out for number one," states the cultural proverb. "If you think it is OK, then it is OK for you," one student tells another in terms of morality, legality, religion, etc. The joy of fellowship among believers that mirrors the joy of fellowship among the divine persons of the Trinity—and results in eternal life—is eclipsed by cultural individualism. It takes lots of conscious effort on the part of those who share communion to keep out individualism. On the Feast of St. John, apostle and evangelist, we accept the challenge of fellowship.

Meditation: In what specific ways do you fellowship with others?

Prayer: In the beginning was your Word, heavenly Father, joined to you in love by the Holy Spirit. Through Jesus Christ, you have shared this fellowship of eternal life with all who believe in him. Through the intercession of St. John, strengthen our unity and remove all individualism that keeps us from sharing what we have heard and seen with others. We ask this through the same Jesus Christ, our Lord, who lives and reigns with you and the Holy Spirit, one God, forever and ever. Amen.

Feast of St. John, Apostle and Evangelist

See and Believe

John 20:1a, 2–8

Scripture: ". . . [T]he other disciple [, the one whom Jesus loved,], who reached the tomb first, also went in, and he saw and believed . . ." (John 20:8).

Reflection: After Joseph of Arimathea is assisted uniquely by Nicodemus in entombing Jesus' body on Friday in John's Gospel, Mary Magdalene goes to the tomb on Sunday morning and sees "that the stone had been removed from the tomb" (20:1). Her conclusion, which she voices to "Simon Peter and the other disciple, the one whom Jesus loved" (20:2), is that someone has "taken the Lord out of the tomb" (20:2). The two recipients of Mary Magdalene's conclusion race toward the tomb. The "other disciple," who is never named, reaches the tomb first, but he waited until Simon Peter arrived so he could enter it first.

In the Johannine community near the end of the first century AD, there seems to be a leadership issue that is reflected in this passage. The "other disciple" must have been the leader of the church which produced this work, even though Peter had gained prominence as leader of all believers as found in the other gospels and the Acts of the Apostles, because he follows Peter into the tomb and sees and believes.

Seeing and believing is a Johannine theme worked throughout the gospel. Jesus gives a sign, and people believe. He changes water into wine at Cana of Galilee, and many believe in him. He restores the sight of a blind man, and many believe in him. He raises Lazarus from the dead, and many believe in him. In John's Gospel, one sees and believes. This theme will be subverted a few verses later with the narrative about Thomas. Once Jesus has finished his work on earth, there are no more signs to see and believe. So, the Johannine authors subvert the theme with Jesus' words to Thomas: "Blessed are those who have not seen and yet have come to believe" (20:29).

The "other disciple" makes four appearances in John's Gospel. He appears first during the meal in which Jesus washes his disciples' feet. After Jesus predicts that one of them will betray him, the narrator declares, "One of his disciples—the one whom Jesus loved—was reclining next to him" (13:23). This incident is recalled by the author of the second ending to John's Gospel, when he writes, "Peter turned and saw the disciple whom

Jesus loved following them; he was the one who had reclined next to Jesus at the supper" (21:20).

This "disciple whom Jesus loved" appears the second time after Jesus' arrest and transport to Caiaphas. "Simon Peter and another disciple followed Jesus" (18:15). This "other disciple, who was known to the high priest, went out, spoke to the woman who guarded the gate, and brought Peter in" (18:16).

His third appearance is at the cross, where the Johannine author refers to him as "the disciple whom [Jesus] loved standing beside [his mother]" (19:26). His fourth appearance is in today's pericope in which he is referred to as "the one whom Jesus loved" (20:2) and as "the other disciple" (20:3–4, 8). In no appearance is he ever named!

It is a bit of liturgical irony that on the Feast of St. John, Apostle and Evangelist, we do not read a passage from John's Gospel that actually names this apostle. But maybe that is the beauty of this feast. We can be the "other disciple" who believes in Christ's resurrection without seeing the sign of the empty tomb and the linen wrappings. The Johannine author prefers faith in the resurrection without signs; we can be "another disciple" who reads the testimony of John's Gospel and believes that God raised Jesus from the dead.

Meditation: What do you believe about your Catholic faith without signs?

Prayer: Ever-living God, as we honor the apostle John, we praise the Holy Spirit for inspiring him to write words that fill us with faith in the resurrection of Christ. Grant that we may join him to see your light and to share in eternal life. You live and reign as one God—Father, Son, and Holy Spirit—forever and ever. Amen.

✤ December 28
Feast of the Holy Innocents, Martyrs

Light

1 John 1:5–2:2

Scripture: "This is the message we have heard from [Jesus Christ] and proclaim to you, that God is light and in him there is no darkness at all" (1 John 1:5).

Reflection: The third day after Christmas is the Feast of the Holy Innocents, martyrs. The first reading is taken from the first Letter of John. Unless a Sunday falls on December 27, today's passage continues where yesterday's prologue left off. Written near the end of the first century AD, 1 John is more like a theological document than a letter. The author, coming out of the same Johannine school as the authors of John's Gospel, contrasts light and darkness.

After declaring that "God is light" (1:5), that is, God has revealed himself as light, the author's logical conclusion is that those who fellowship with him share in that light just as Jesus "himself is in the light" (1:7). It is impossible for people to "have fellowship with him while [they] are walking in darkness" (1:6). In other words, light and dark cannot exist together simultaneously.

Furthermore, whatever sin people may have had has been cleansed by "the blood of Jesus" (1:7). All they need to do is confess their sins, and he will forgive them. "If [they] say that [they] have no sin, [they] deceive [them]selves, and the truth is not in [them]" (1:8). And, "If [they] say that [they] have not sinned, [they] make him a liar, and his word is not in [them]" (1:10).

Sin, by its very nature, is self-deceiving. Entering into fellowship with God and Jesus Christ shines light on sin to reveal its true nature. Once sin is seen in the light of God, the blood of Jesus washes away its darkness. "Jesus Christ the righteous" (2:1) serves as an advocate with the Father for any who sin. He is "the atoning sacrifice for . . . sins, . . . for the sins of the whole world." (2:2).

The darkness of sin is seen in Herod, who desires to destroy the light of Jesus. Joseph, Mary, and Jesus flee during the night to Egypt to escape Herod's massacre of children in and around Bethlehem two years old or younger. The same darkness engulfs those mothers who abort their children, those men and women who abuse children, those young men and women who bully others. The way to see sin is to shine God's light on it.

Meditation: What light of God have you recently seen shine on sin?

Prayer: Almighty Father, through the sacrifice of Jesus, your Son, you have shed your light on the whole world. Make us aware of our darkness, and, through the Holy Spirit, help us confess our sinfulness, that we may experience the light that the blood of Jesus Christ has won for us. He is Lord forever and ever. Amen.

Witnesses

Matthew 2:13–18

Scripture: "When Herod saw that he had been tricked by the wise men, he was infuriated, and he sent and killed all the children in and around Bethlehem who were two years old or under, according to the time that he had learned from the wise men" (Matt 2:16).

Reflection: This biblical Feast of the Holy Innocents appears only in Matthew's Gospel after the unique narrative about the wise men or magi from the East make a pilgrimage through Jerusalem to Bethlehem to pay homage to the newborn king of the Jews. Several Matthean motifs are presented in today's six-verse pericope.

Feast of the Holy Innocents, Martyrs

God has everything under control and manages it through dreams. The magi are "warned in a dream not to return to Herod" (2:12). An "angel of the Lord appeared to Joseph in a dream" (2:13) and tells him to take Mary and Jesus to Egypt. After Herod dies, "an angel of the Lord suddenly appears in a dream to Joseph in Egypt" (2:19) and tells him to take his family to the land of Israel. The first two chapters of Matthew's Gospel are filled with the dream motif; it is how God unfolds his plan for the salvation of Jews and Gentiles.

Another Matthean motif is the prediction-fulfillment one. The author of this gospel likes to predict that something will happen and then narrate that it did happen—in order to fulfill a Hebrew Bible (Old Testament) quote. In today's passage, the angel of the Lord tells Joseph that "Herod is about to search for the child [Jesus] to destroy him" (2:13). Three verses later, the narrator records that Herod "killed all the children in and around Bethlehem who were two years old or under" (2:16). This motif is woven throughout Matthew's Gospel, but is used extensively in the first two chapters.

The use of the Hebrew Bible (Old Testament) appears as being fulfilled two times in today's passage. The narrator explains that Joseph took Mary and Jesus to Egypt and remained there in order "to fulfill what had been spoken by the Lord through the prophet, 'Out of Egypt I have called my son'" (2:15). The out-of-context quote comes from a part of a verse from Hosea: "When Israel was a child, I loved him, and out of Egypt I called my son" (11:1). It refers to the Exodus.

Another Hebrew Bible (Old Testament) out-of-context verse is quoted by the author of Matthew's Gospel after Herod has all two-year-old and under children killed in and around Bethlehem. This time the narrator gives the source of the quote as the prophet Jeremiah: "Thus says the LORD: A voice is heard in Ramah, lamentation and bitter weeping. Rachel is weeping for her children; she refuses to be comforted for her children, because they are no more" (31:15). The quote refers to the destruction of Jerusalem by King Nebuchadnezzar of Babylon in 587 BC. Rachel was one of the patriarch Jacob's wives who was the mother of Joseph and Benjamin and died in childbirth and was buried near Bethlehem.

The focus of today's feast is the martyrdom of the Holy Innocents by Herod. Matthew's account echoes the beginning of the Book of Exodus in which is told the story of Pharaoh who ordered that all male babies be thrown into the Nile River and killed. Only one escapes, and he is named

Moses, who leads his people out of slavery to freedom. Matthew's portrayal of Joseph taking Jesus to Egypt reveals that the author understands Jesus to be a new Moses, who will free his people from their sins.

The children are hailed as martyrs because they, in their unique Matthean manner, bear witness to Jesus. Considered to be Christian martyrs, the Feast of the Holy Innocents enters the liturgical calendar in the late fifth century AD. It is a reminder that even children can witness the Christian faith. The ranks of the Holy Innocents are still swelling today. Those who abort children, those who abuse children, those who bully children are new Herods who add to the childhood martyrs.

Meditation: What aspect of this feast captures your attention?

Prayer: All-powerful God, you choose the weak and make them strong in bearing witness to you. As we celebrate the Feast of the Holy Innocents, strengthen our faith in your Son, Jesus Christ, that we may be his witnesses throughout the world. We ask this through the same Jesus Christ, who lives and reigns with you and the Holy Spirit, one God, forever and ever. Amen.

www.ingramcontent.com/pod-product-compliance
Lightning Source LLC
Chambersburg PA
CBHW051939160426
43198CB00013B/2215